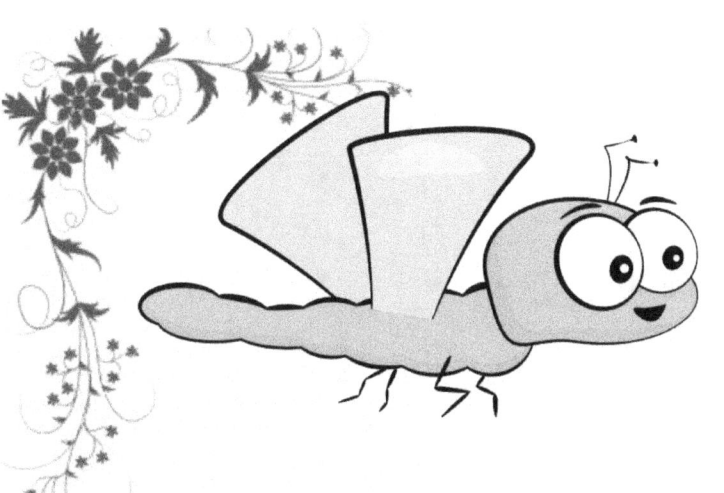

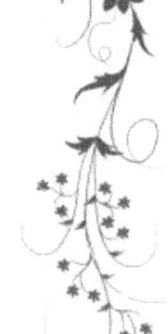

I0475945

Funny Animals. Coloring Book for Kids

Copyright © 2017 by Emily Green

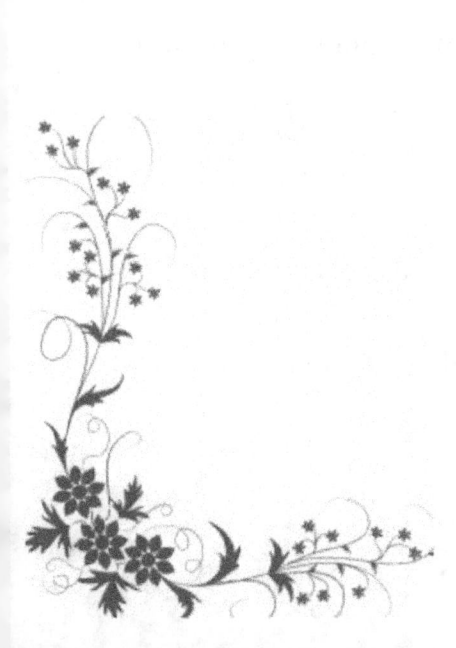

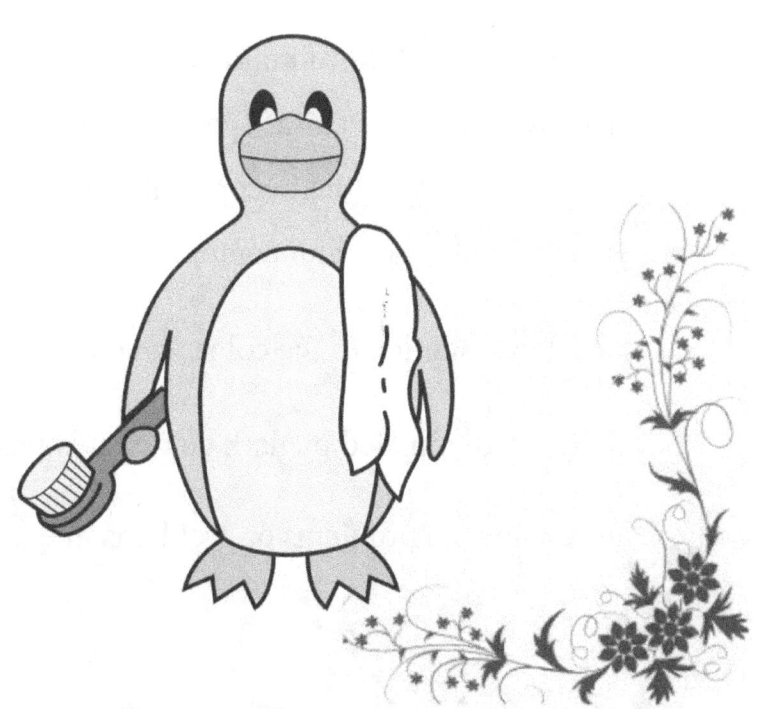

Kids Coloring - this is one of the simplest

and most affordable ways to interest

and usefully spend time. So that gives kids coloring pictures?

Coloring an object, known or unknown to himself, the child completes their knowledge about the shape, the color of the object, develops observation. Initially, the figure and the sun can be green, and orange crocodile. **This is normal**: the child learns, takes him on a piece of paper, trying to reproduce color. By these actions, it expands their horizons.

As a child growing up and development of technology coloring amount of fine detail in the picture is increased, and the figure itself becomes more complex.

In addition to developing motor skills and volitional baby: because he has to try very hard not to go beyond the boundaries of the drawing, you need to learn to control the pressure of a pencil, so as not to tear the paper. **Coloring develops perseverance and attention to the child**.

Teach your child to make a choice. When the choice is made, the remaining coloring take away from the child. Teach your child to bring the follow through. If you notice that the child is unable to cope with the coloring, the next time you ask them a simple picture that he can paint completely.

P.S. Pay attention to the color, which selects the child to colorize. If your child's

picture is dominated by dark colors, it is possible that the child has some

psychological problems or problems in education.

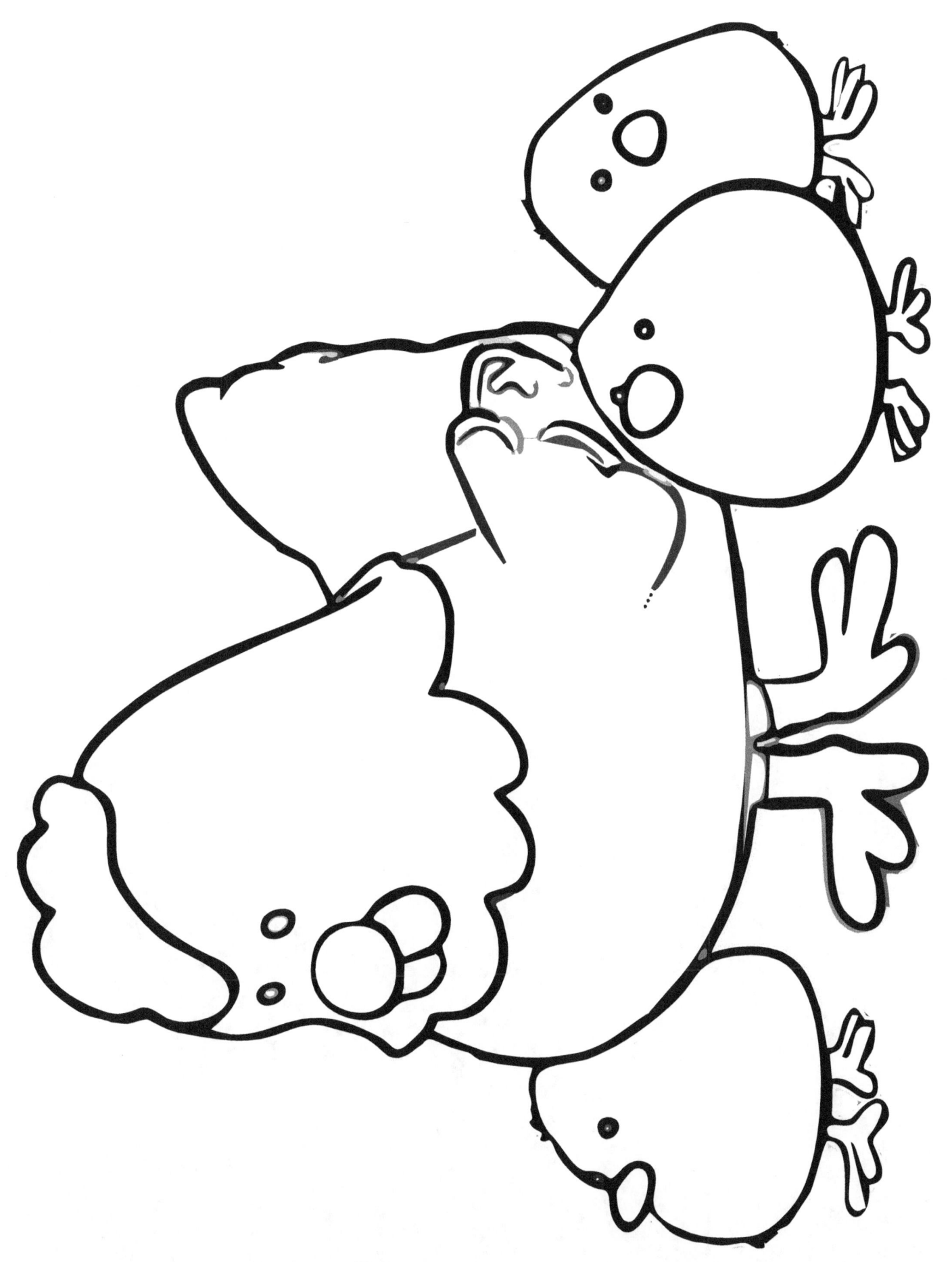

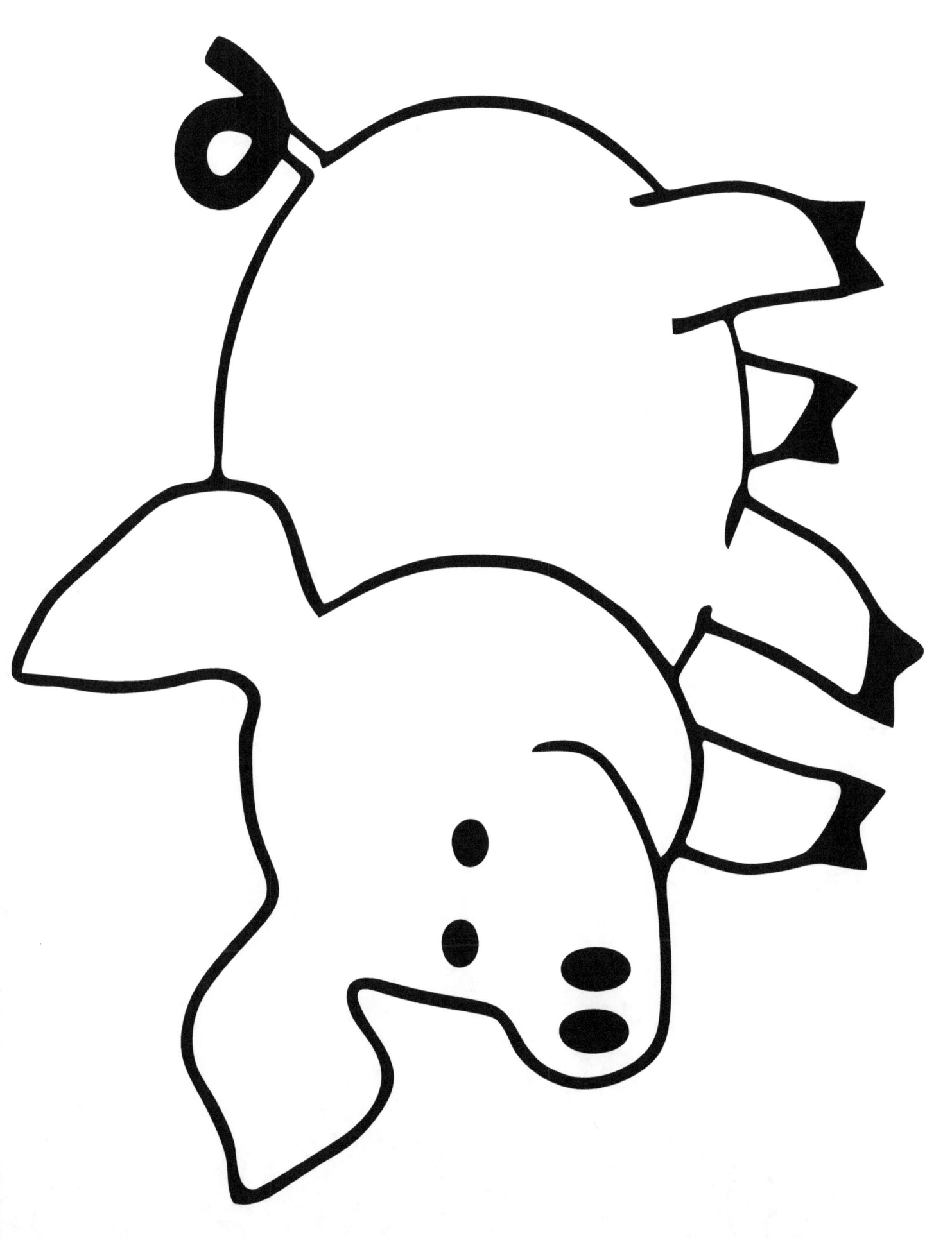

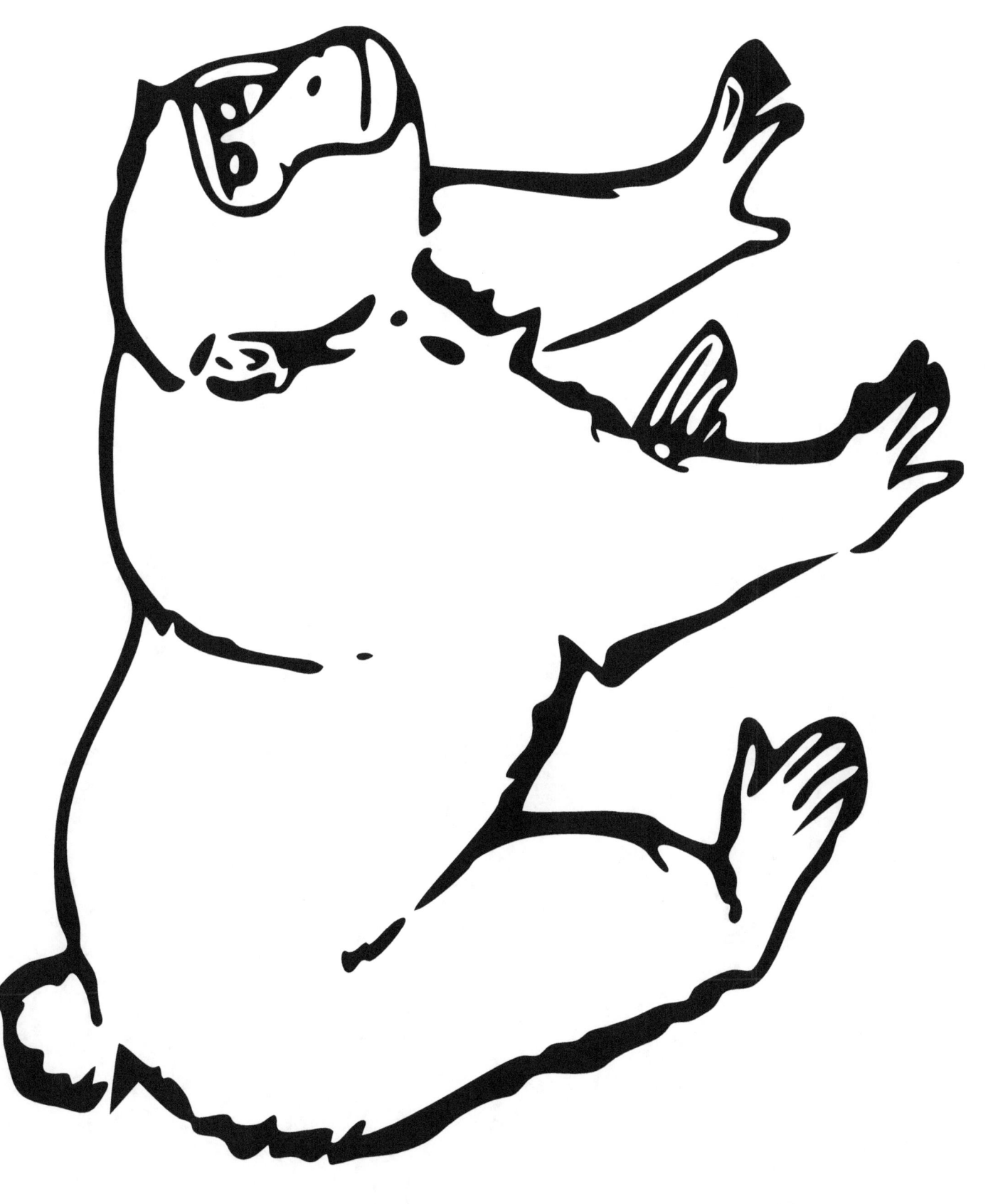

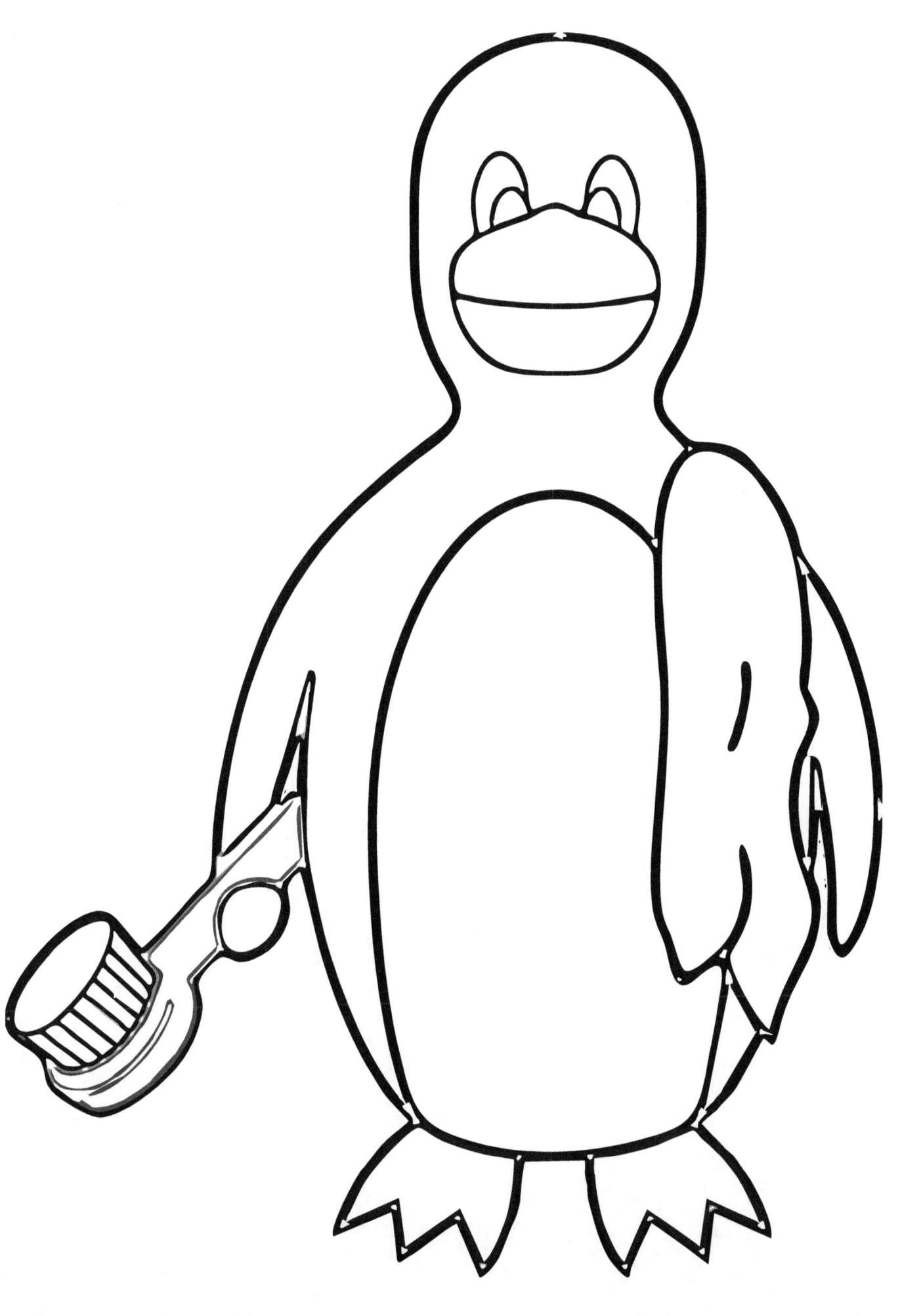

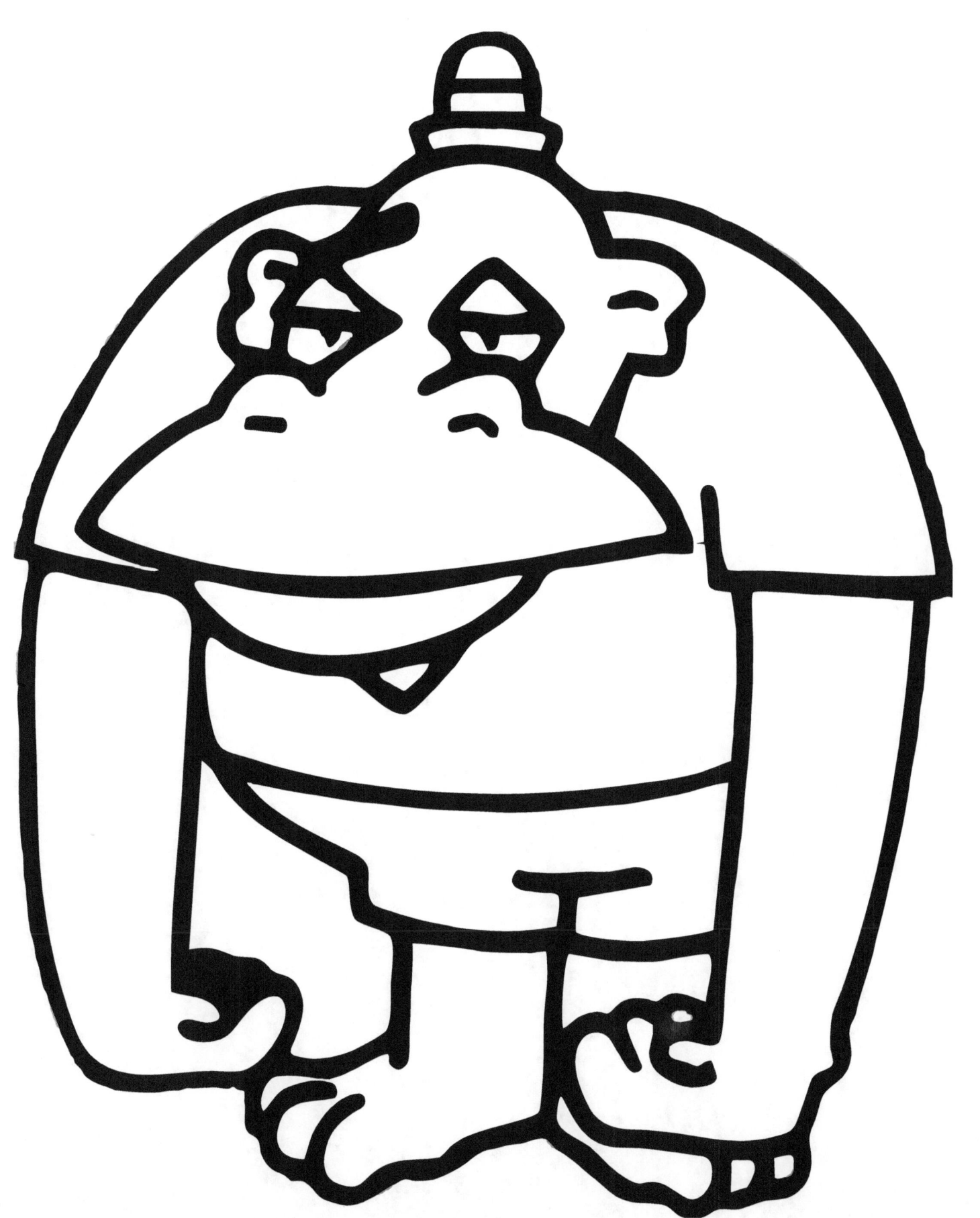

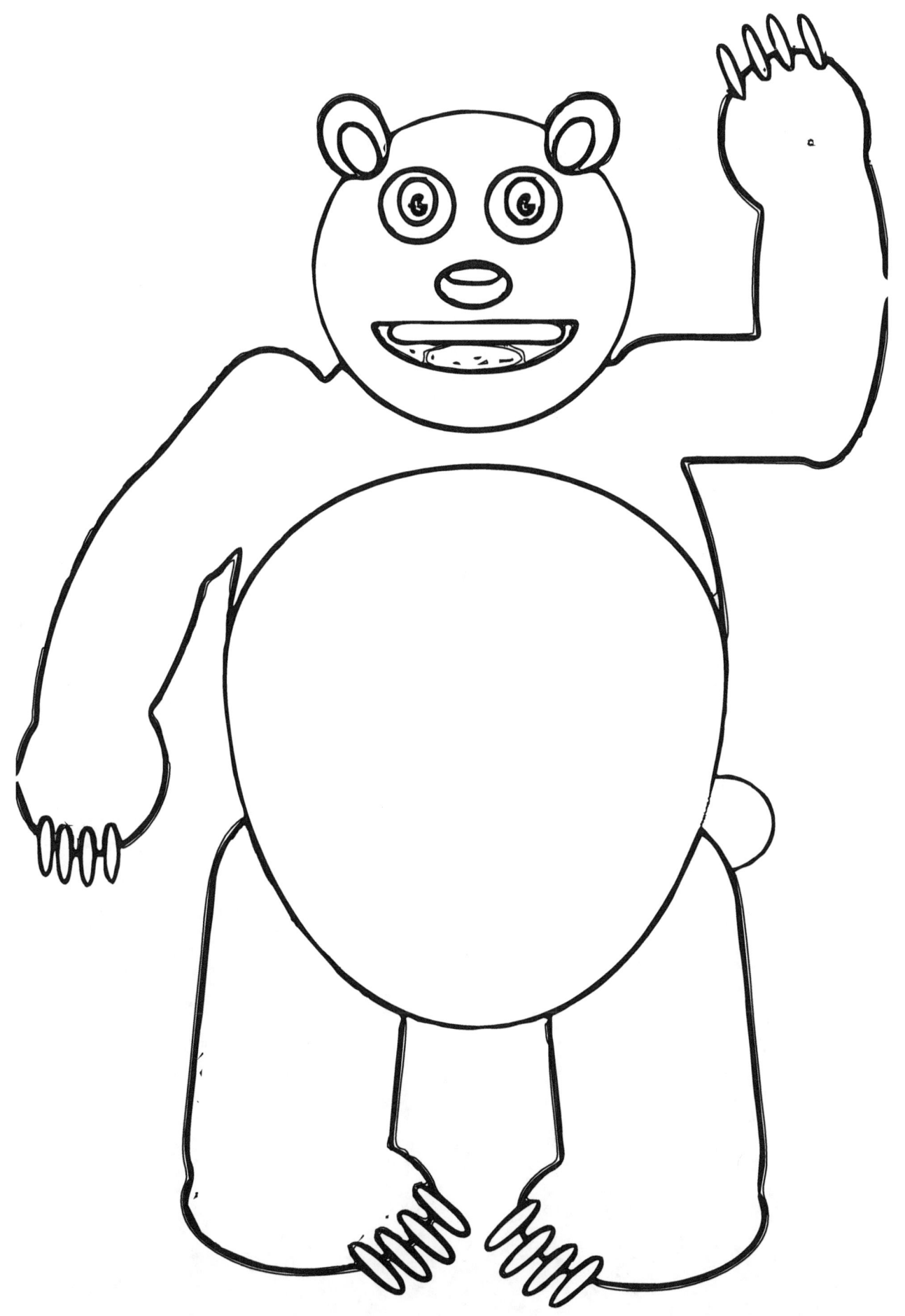

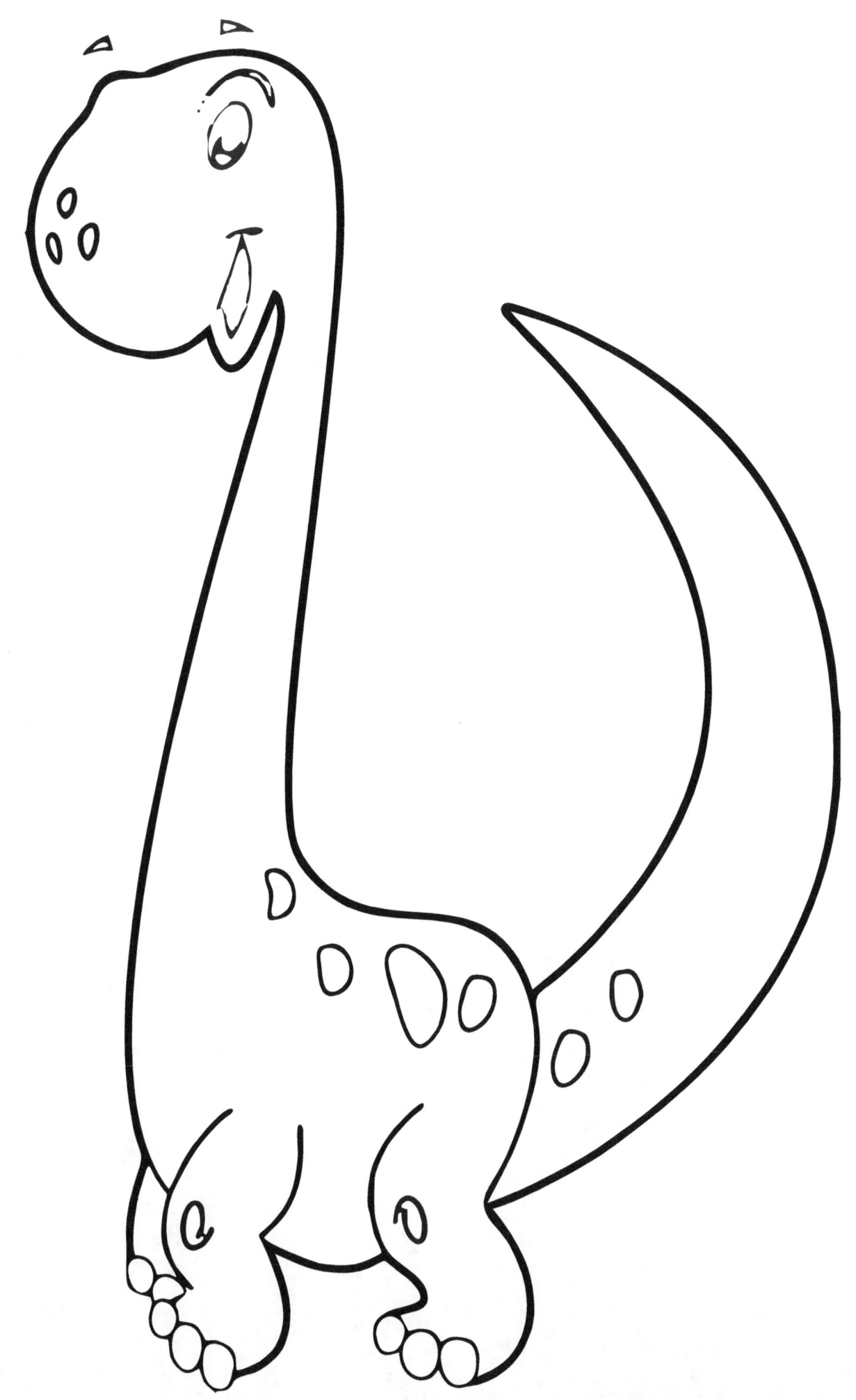

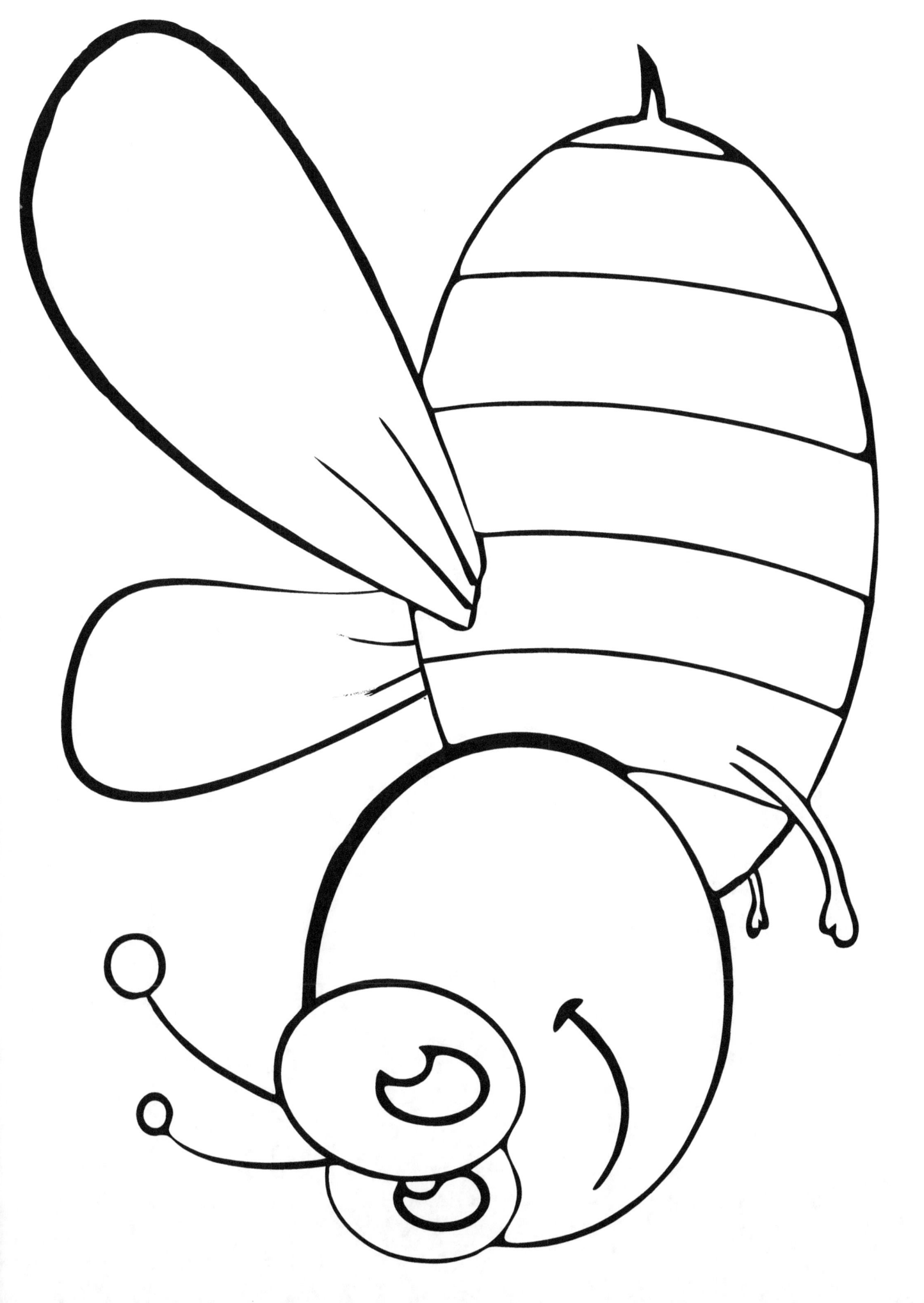

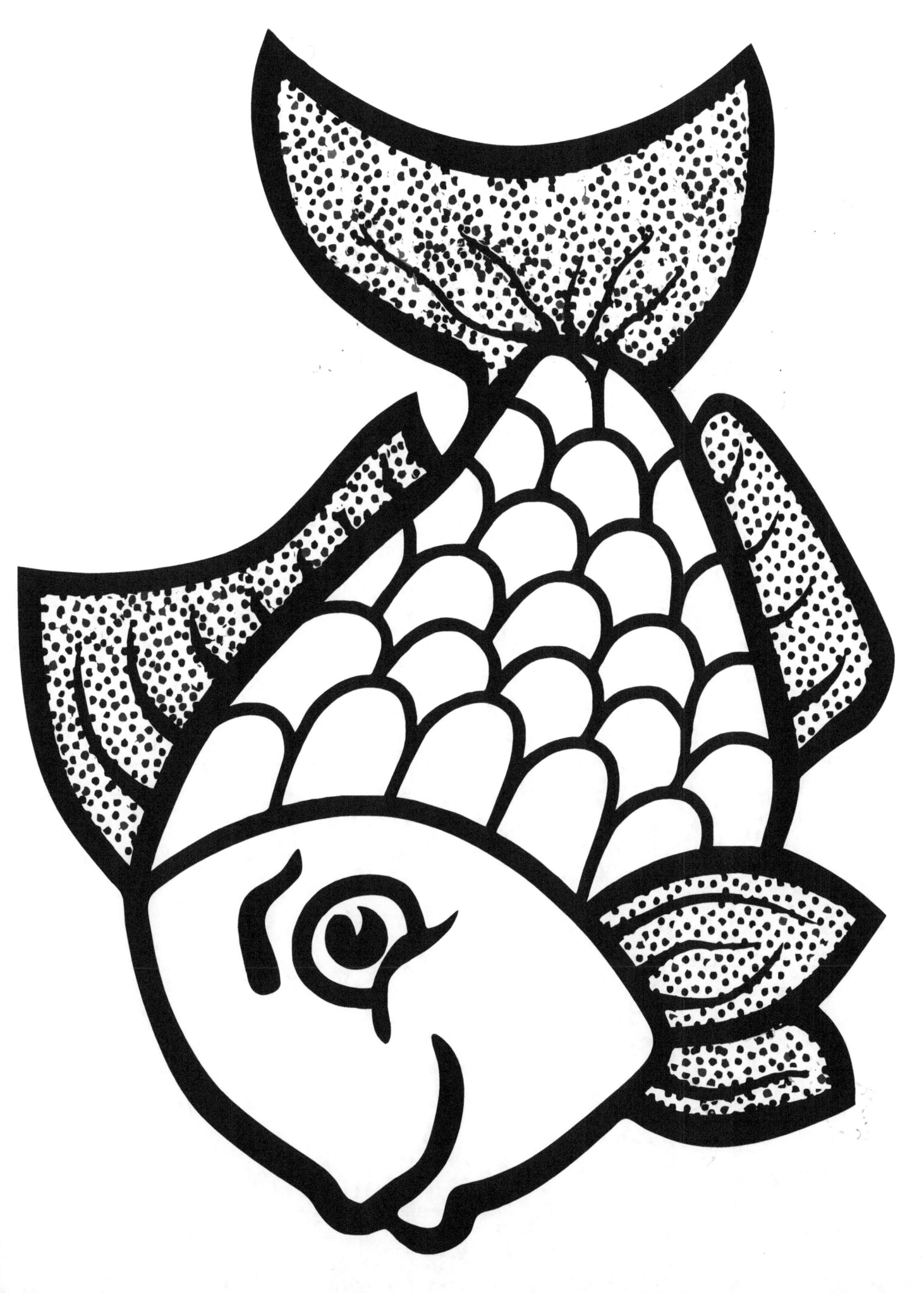

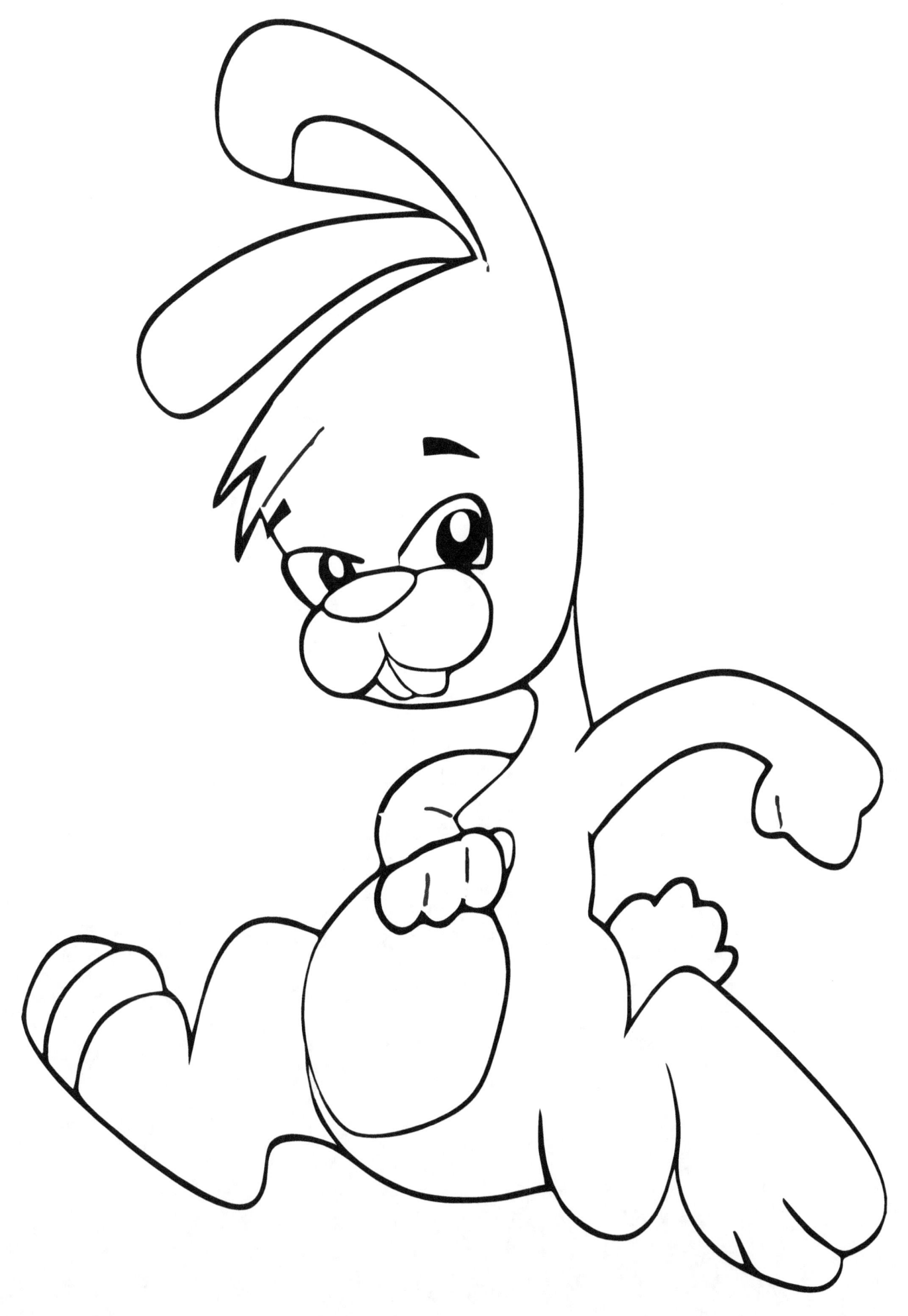

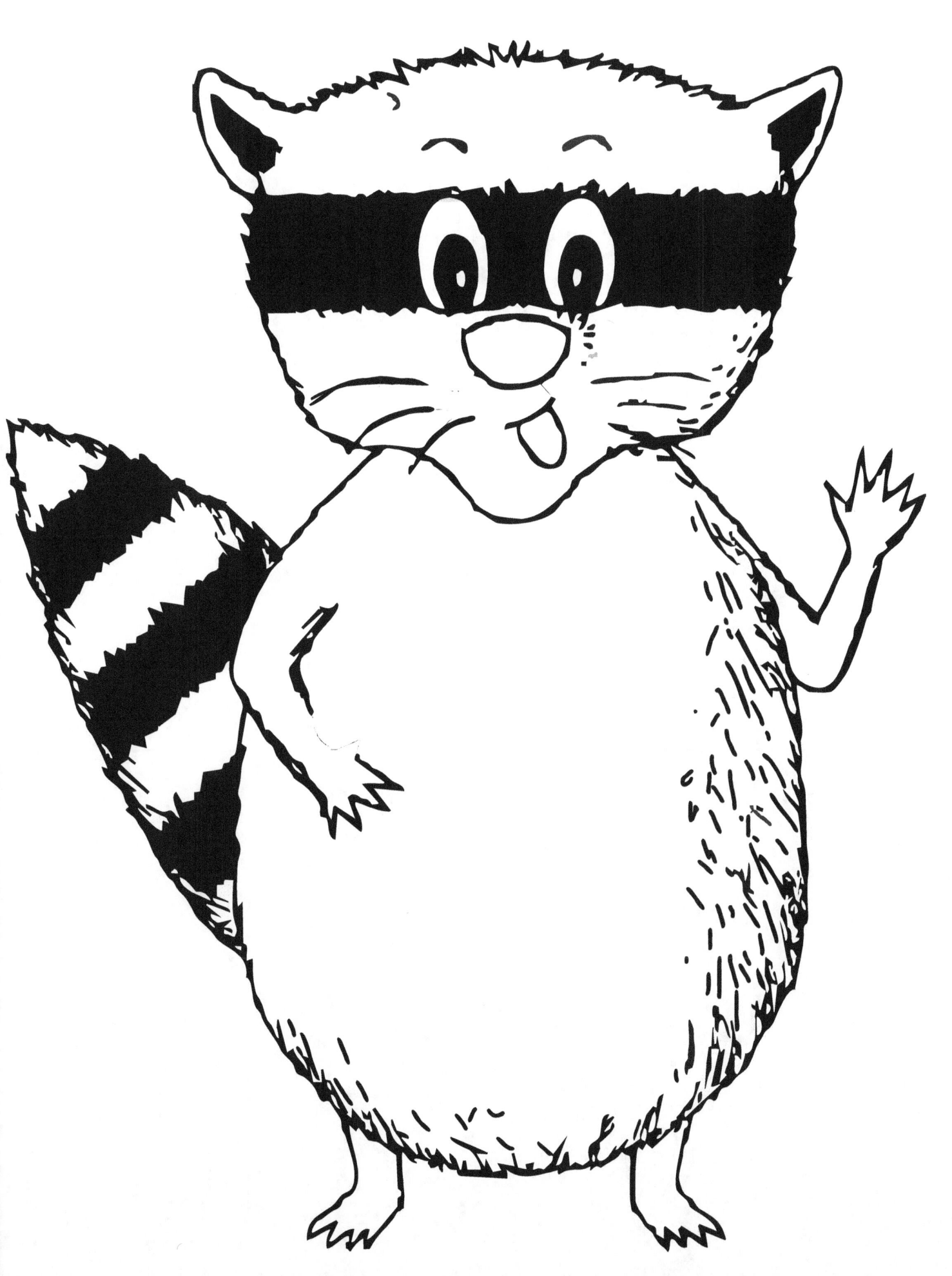

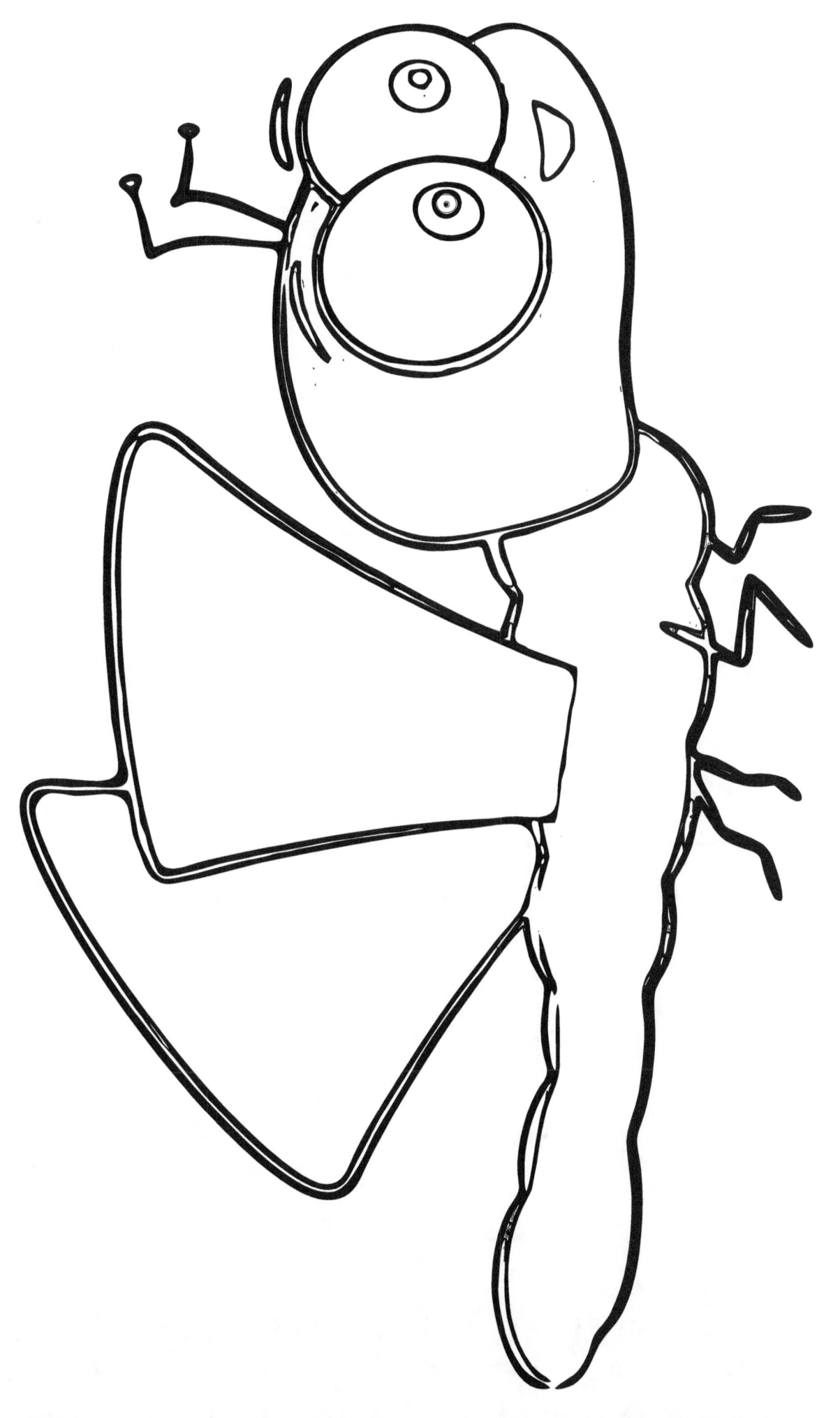

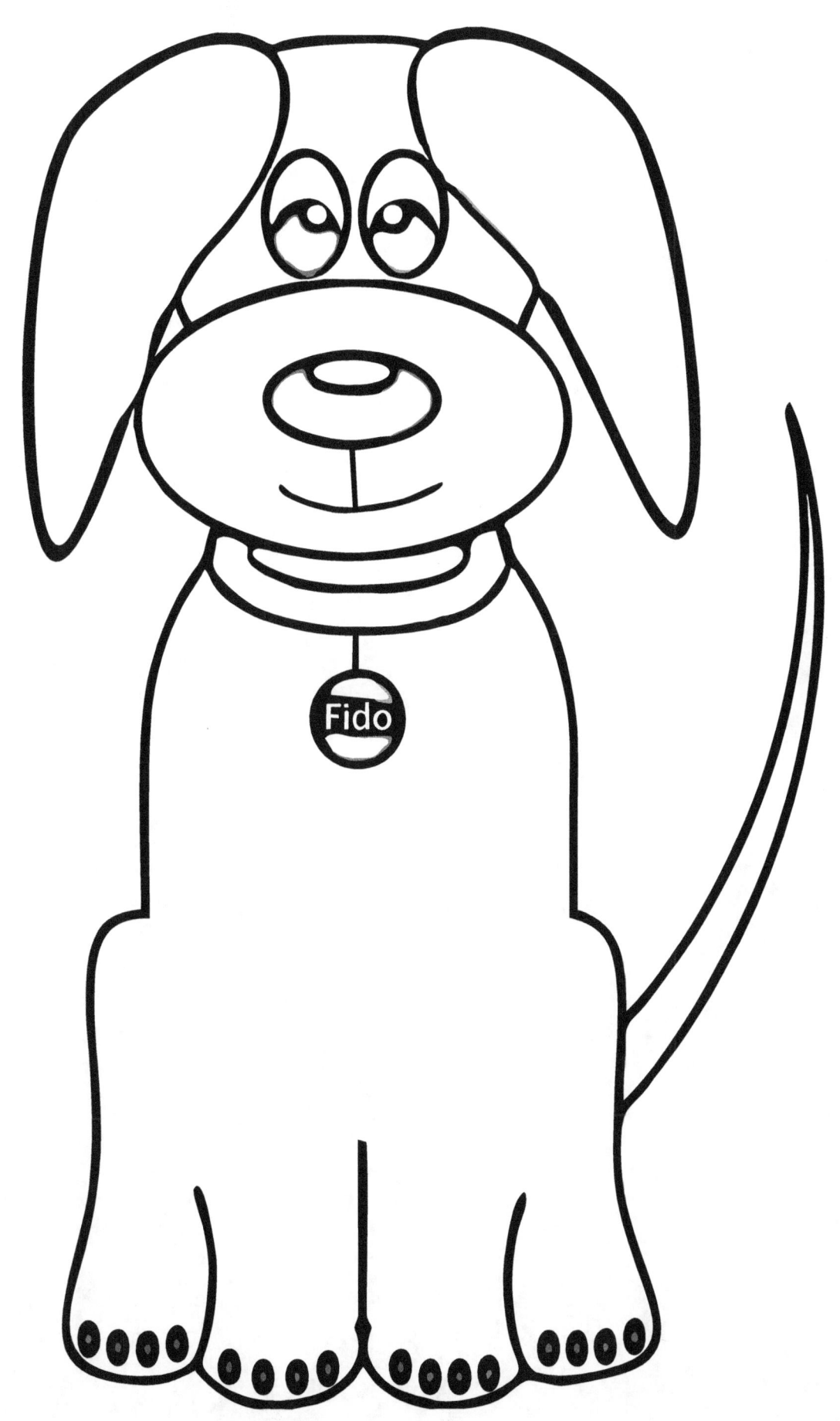

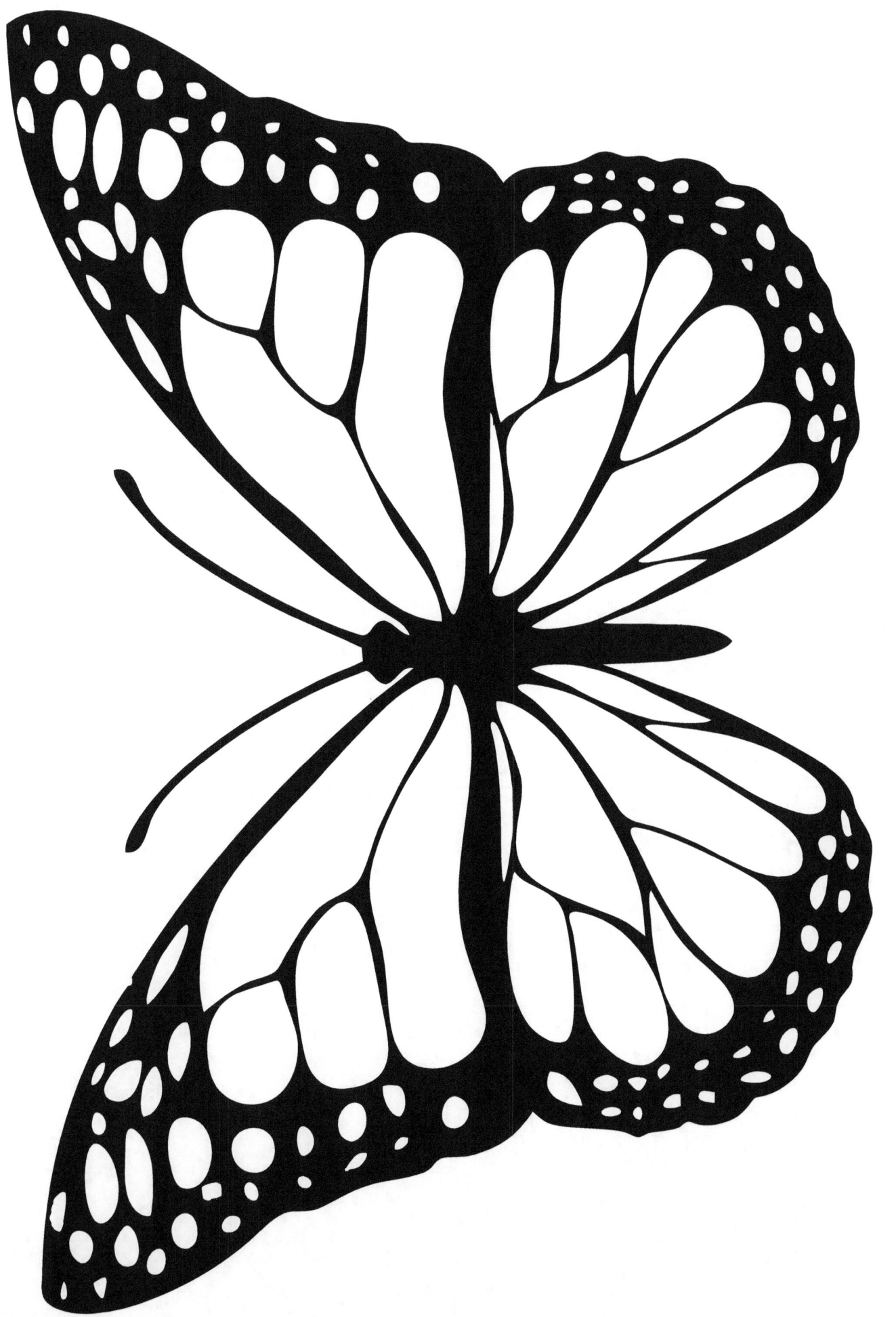

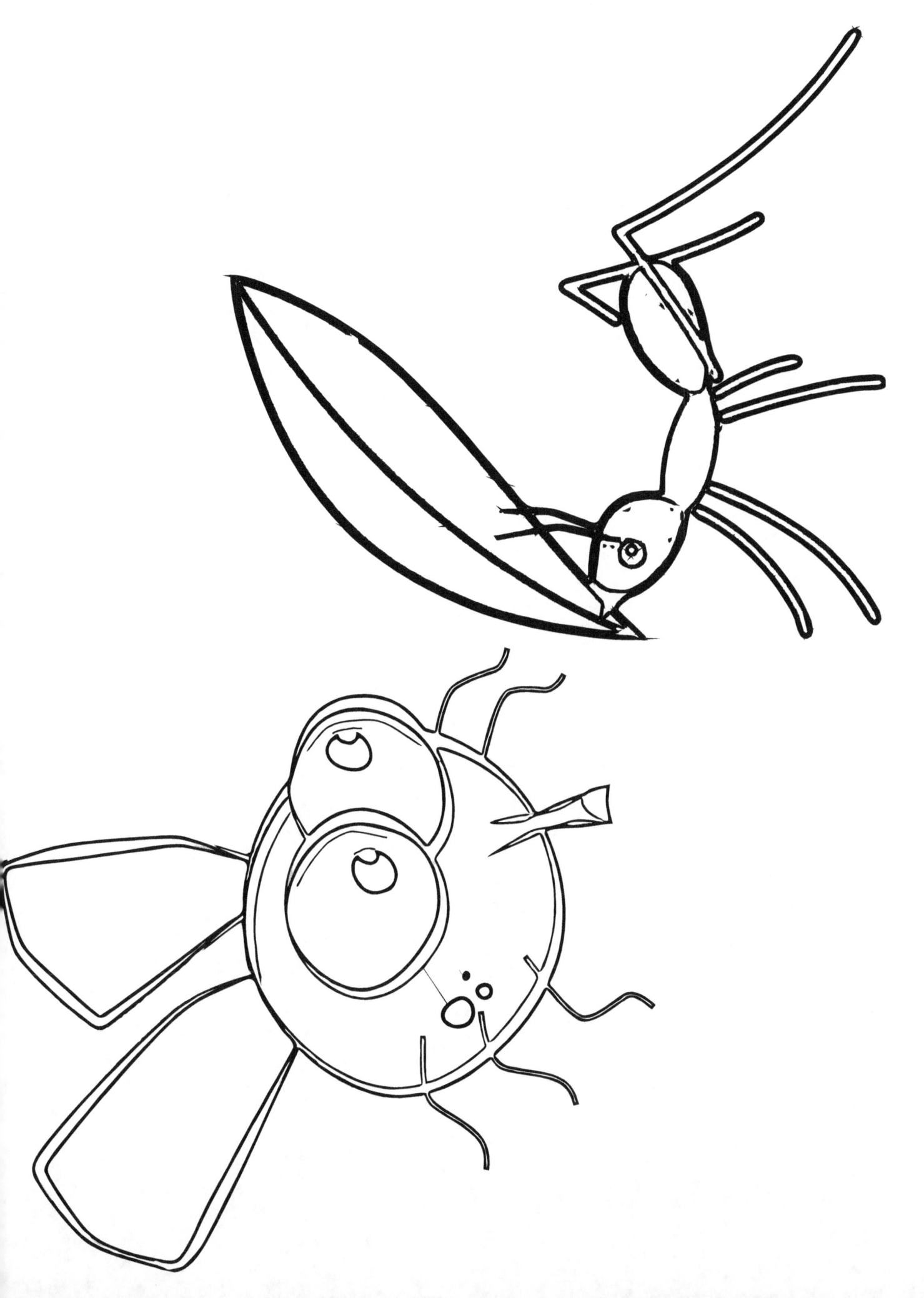

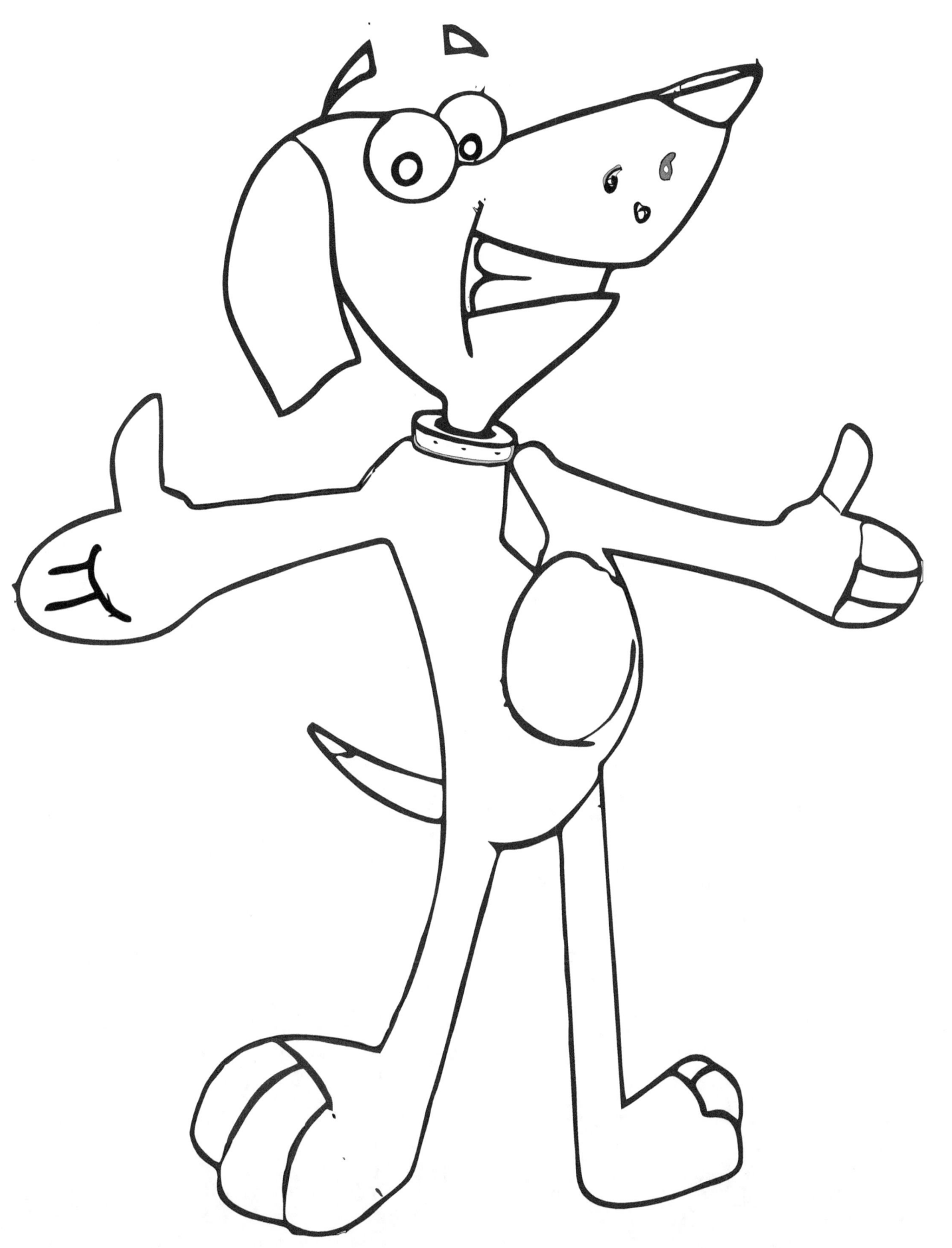

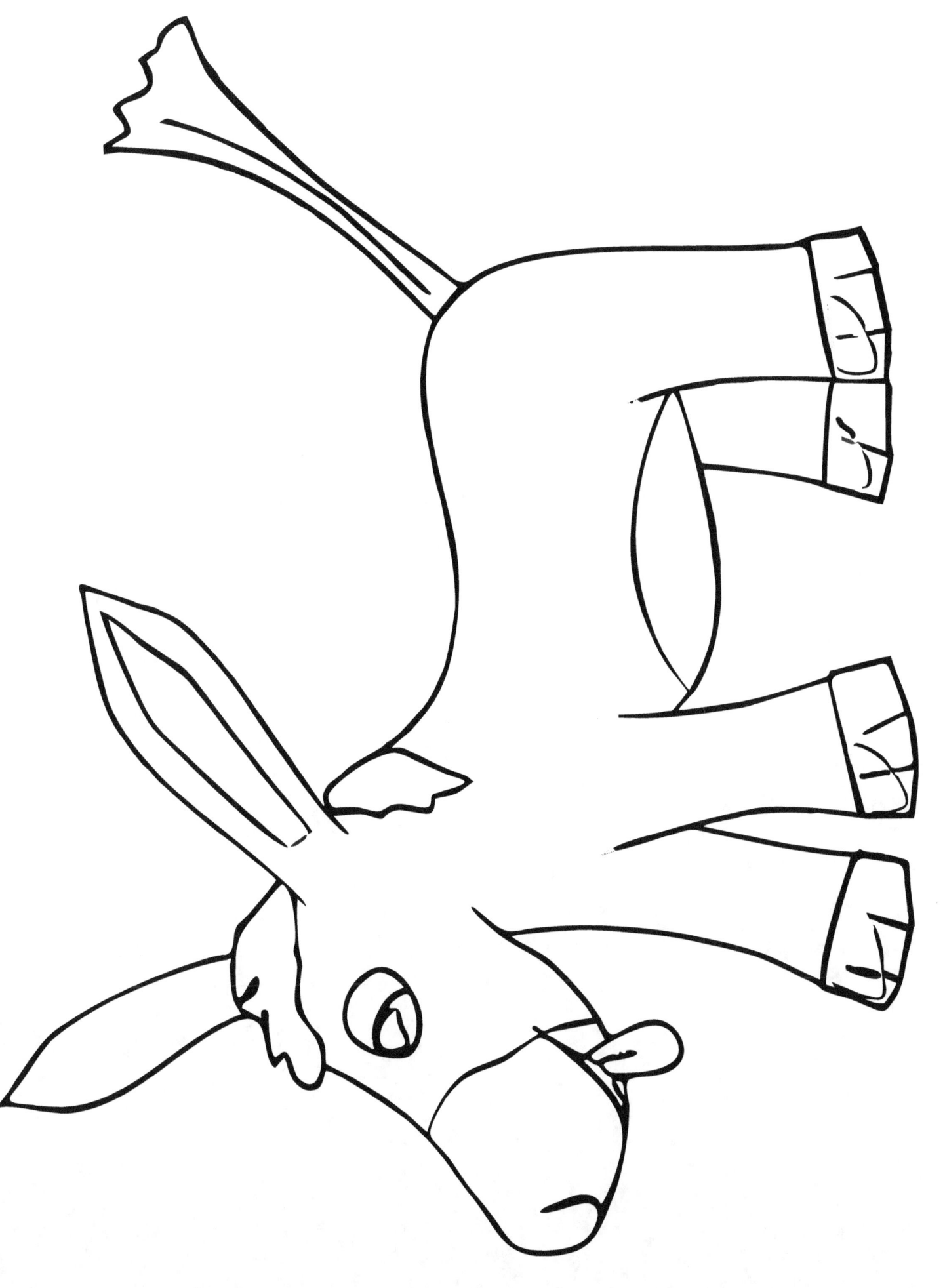

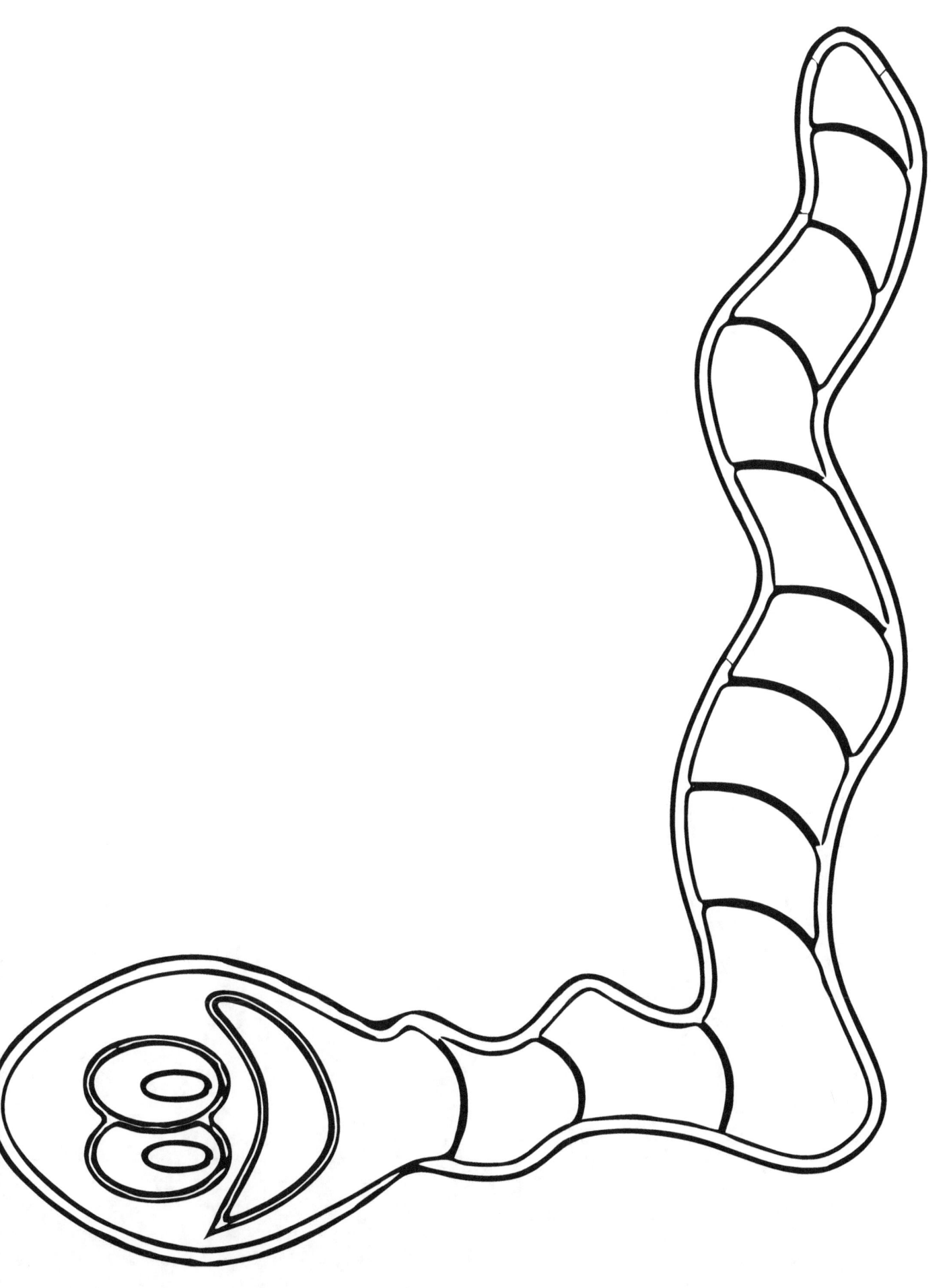

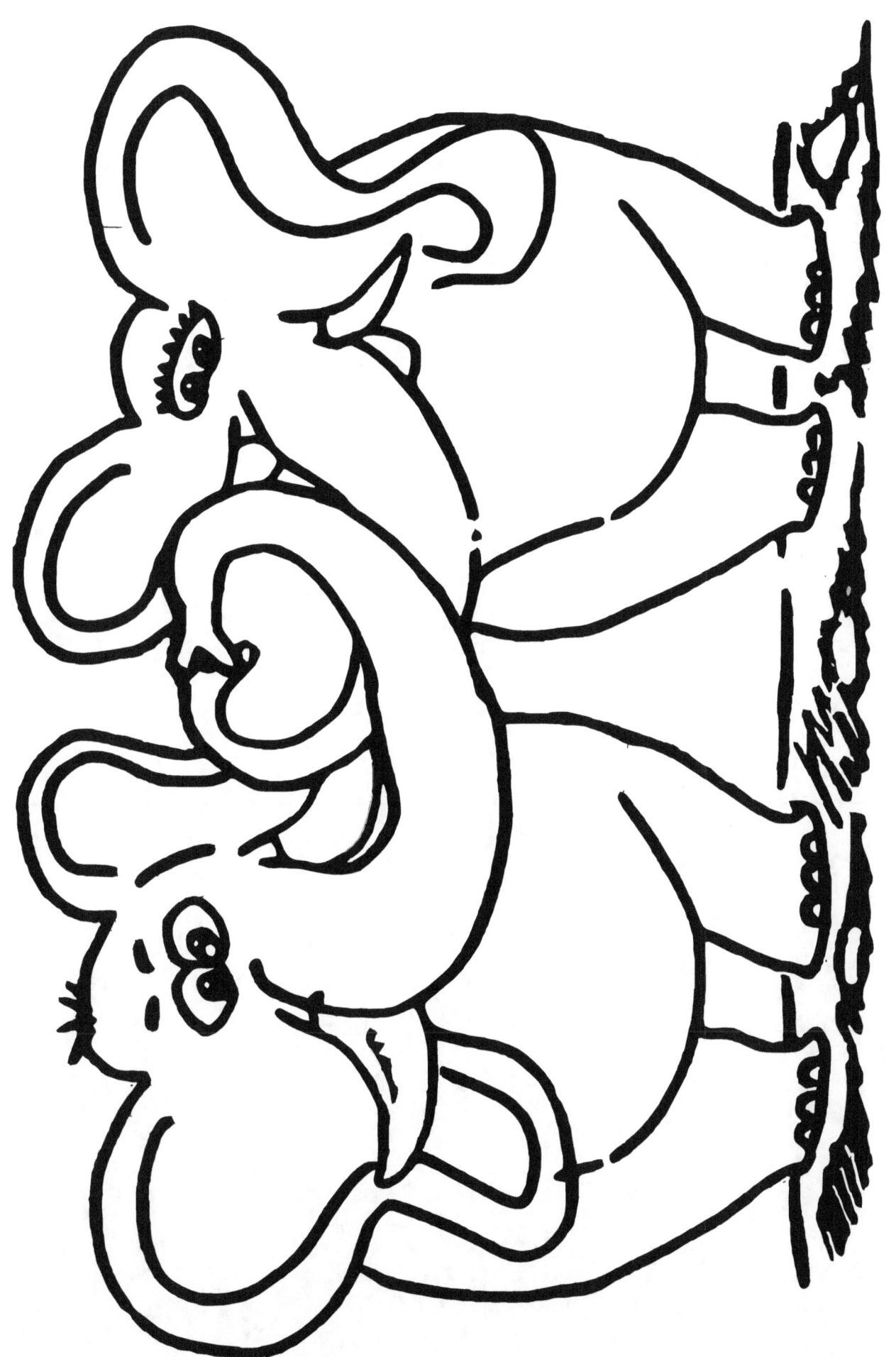

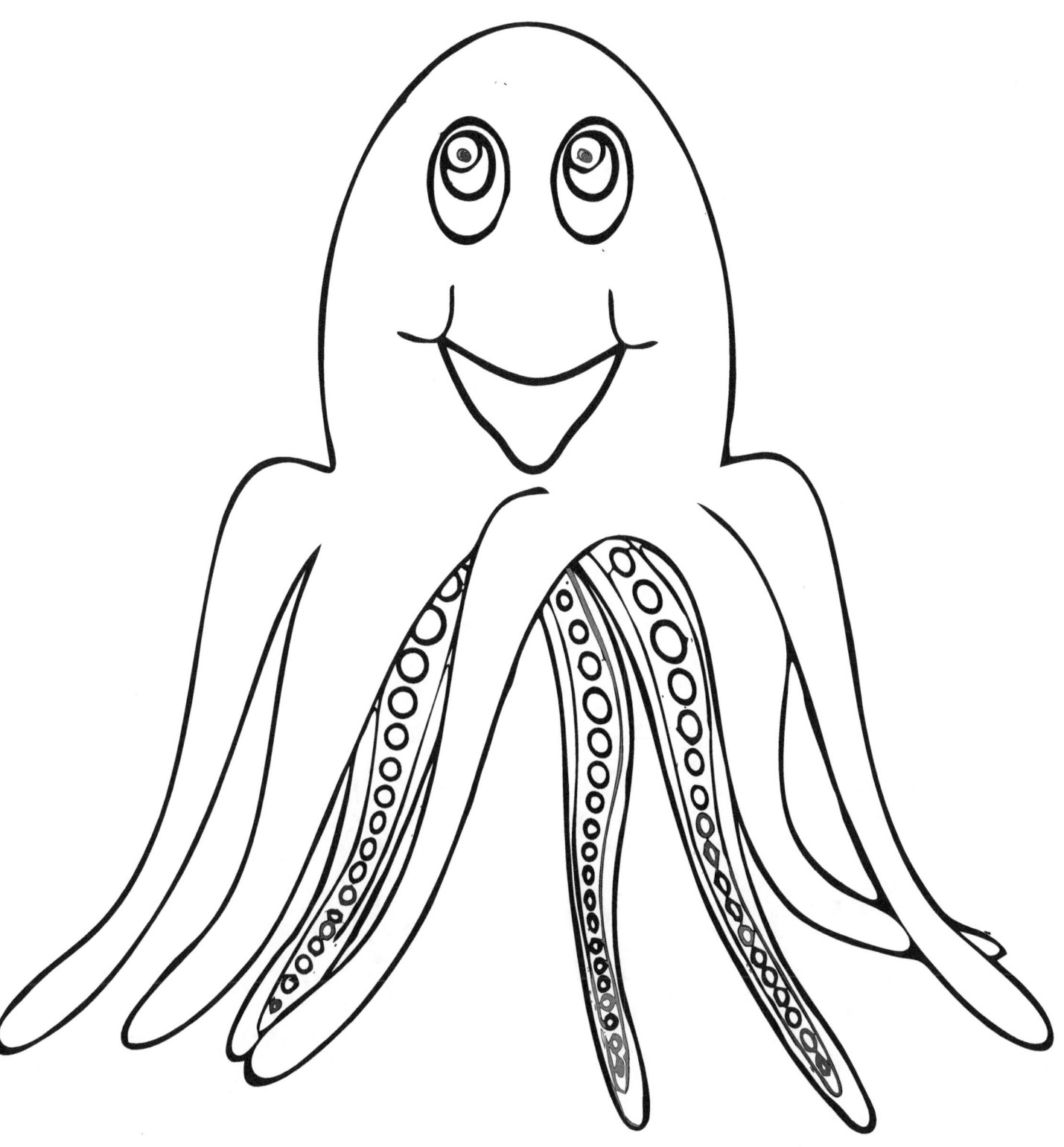

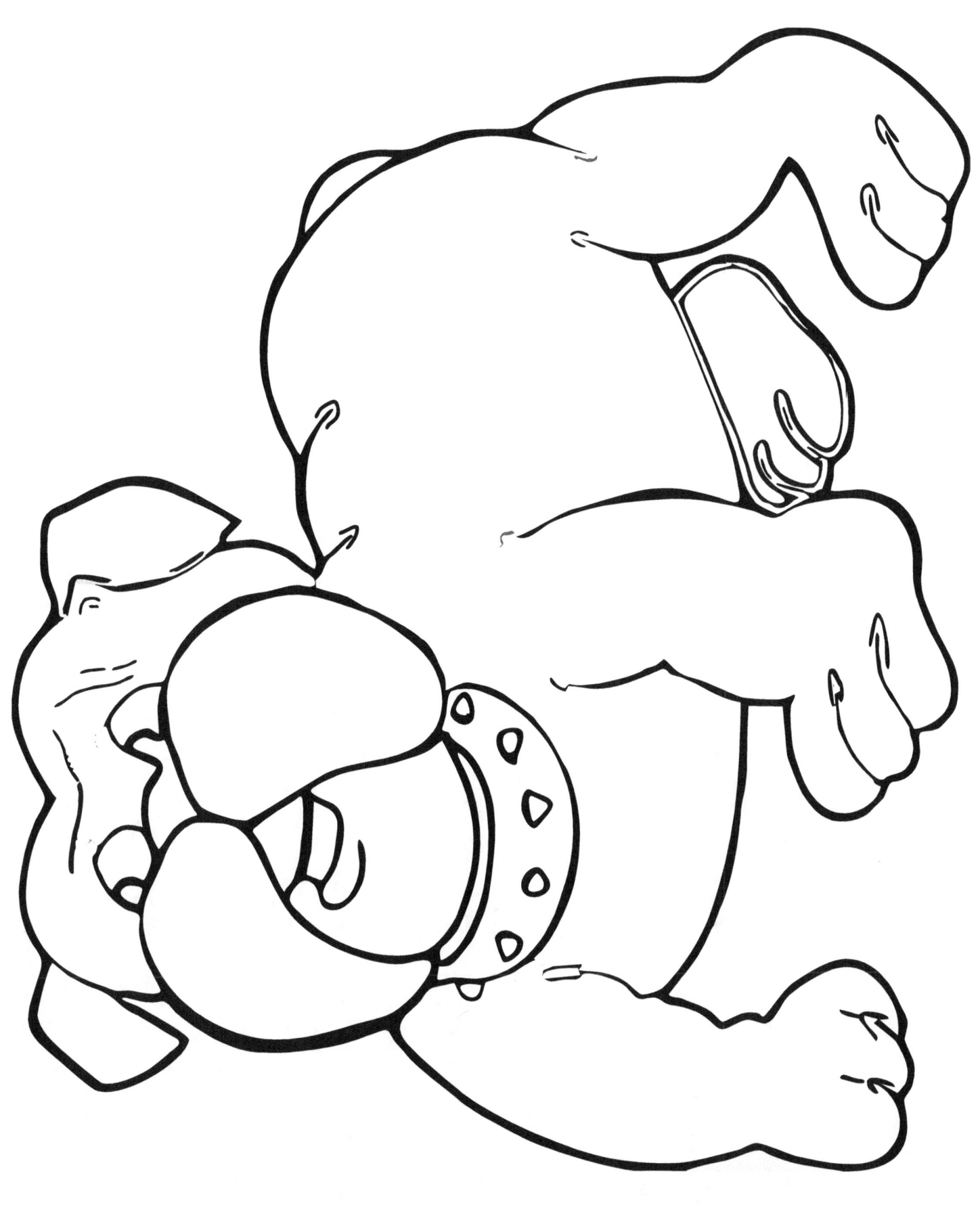

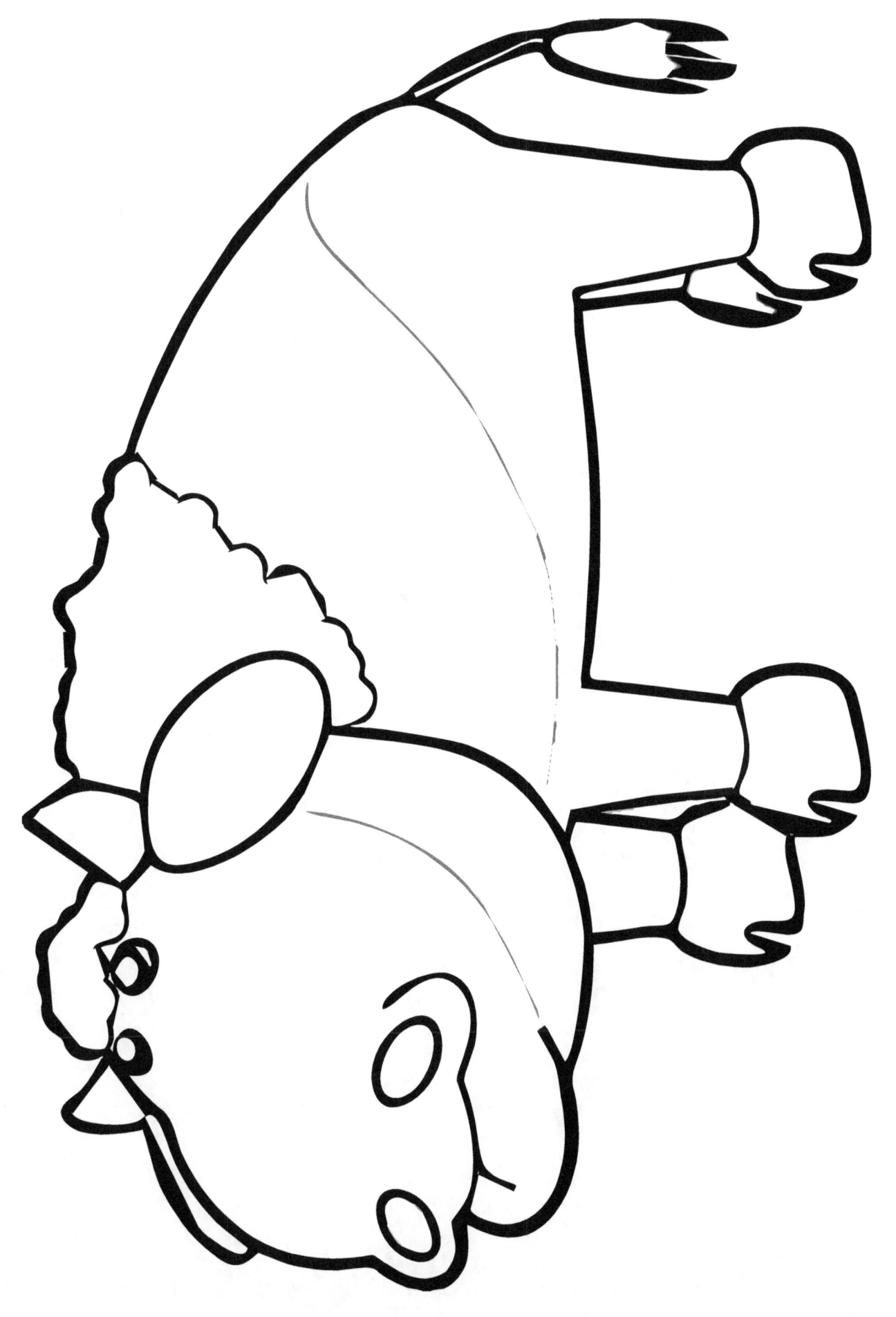

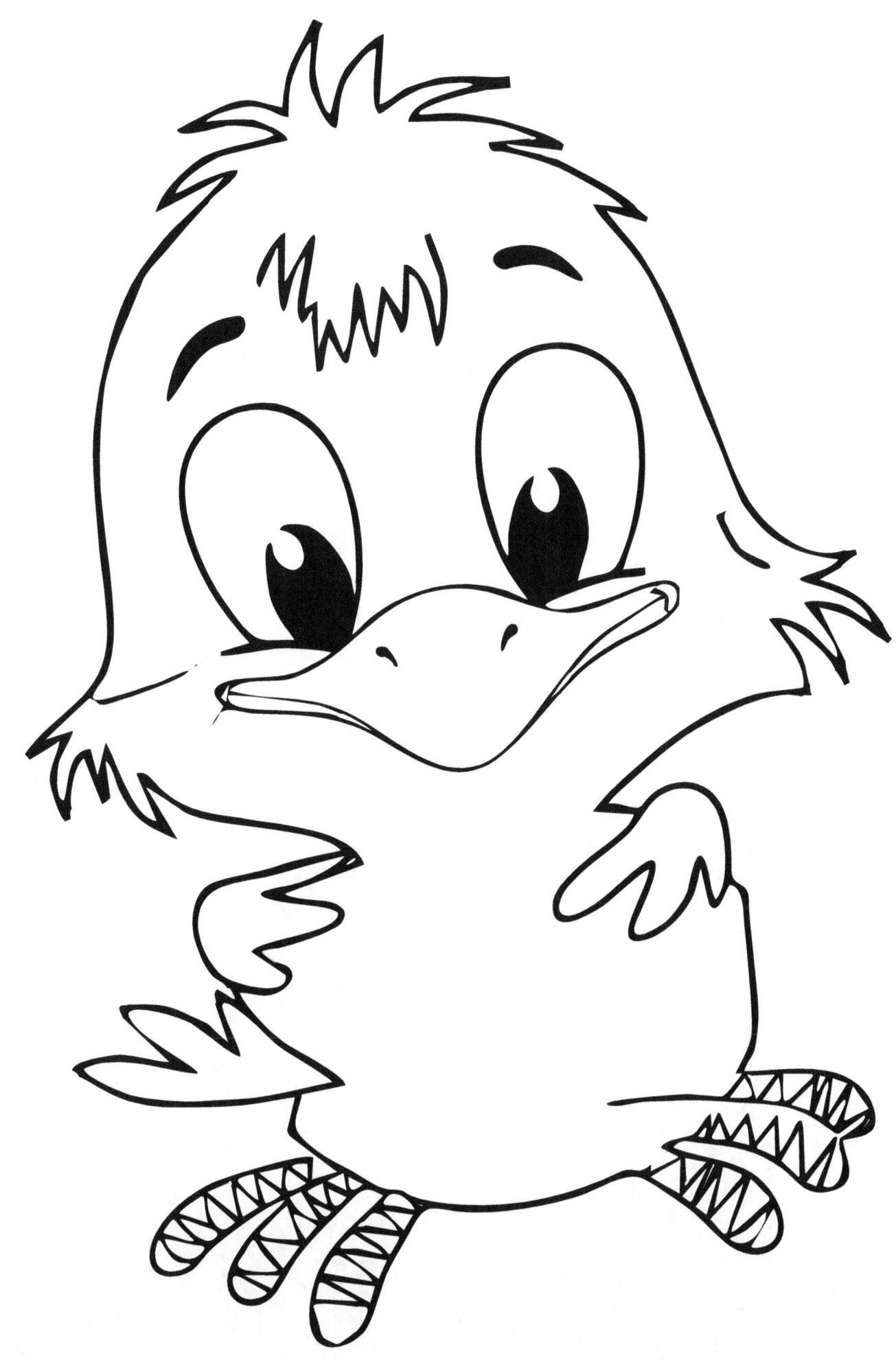

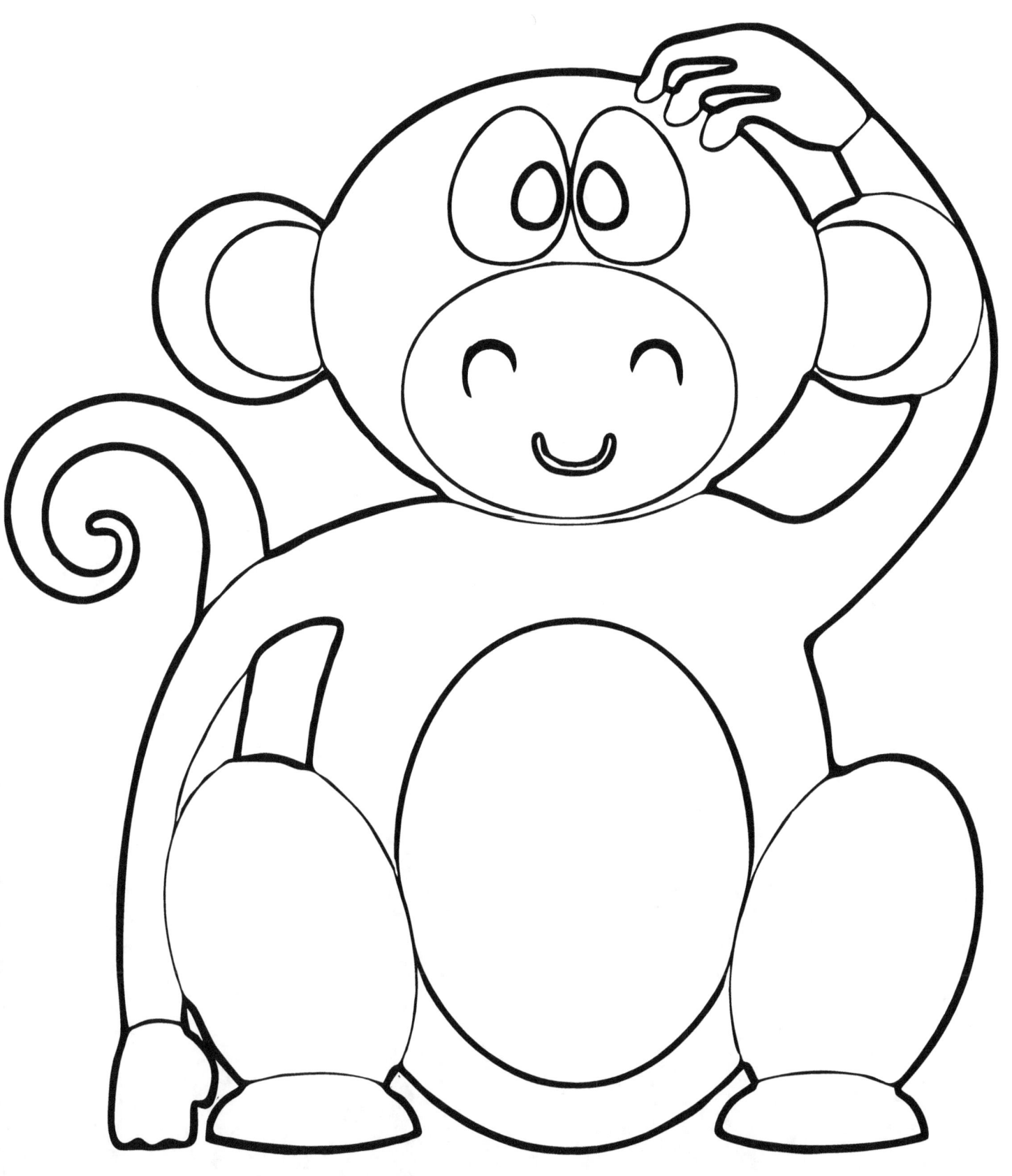

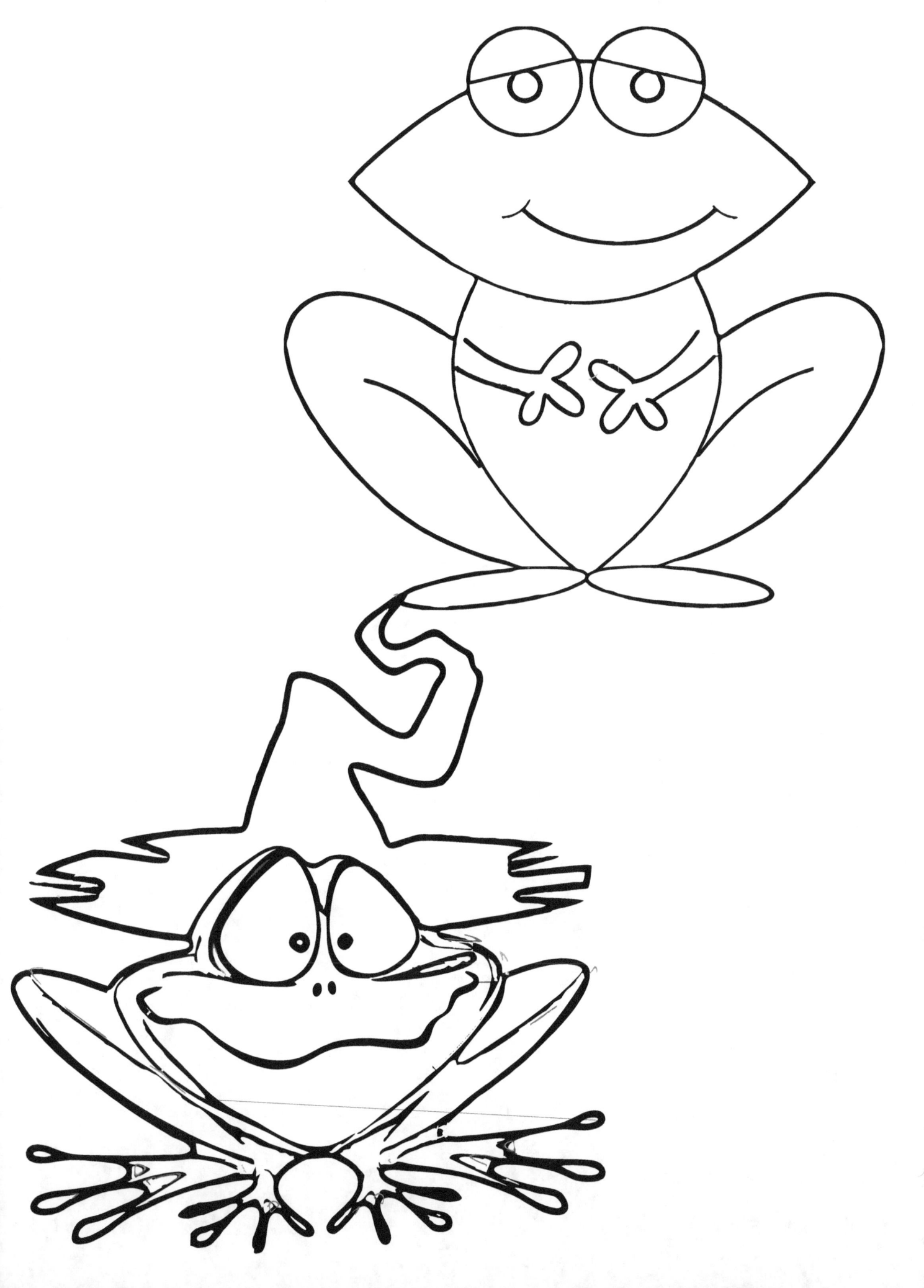

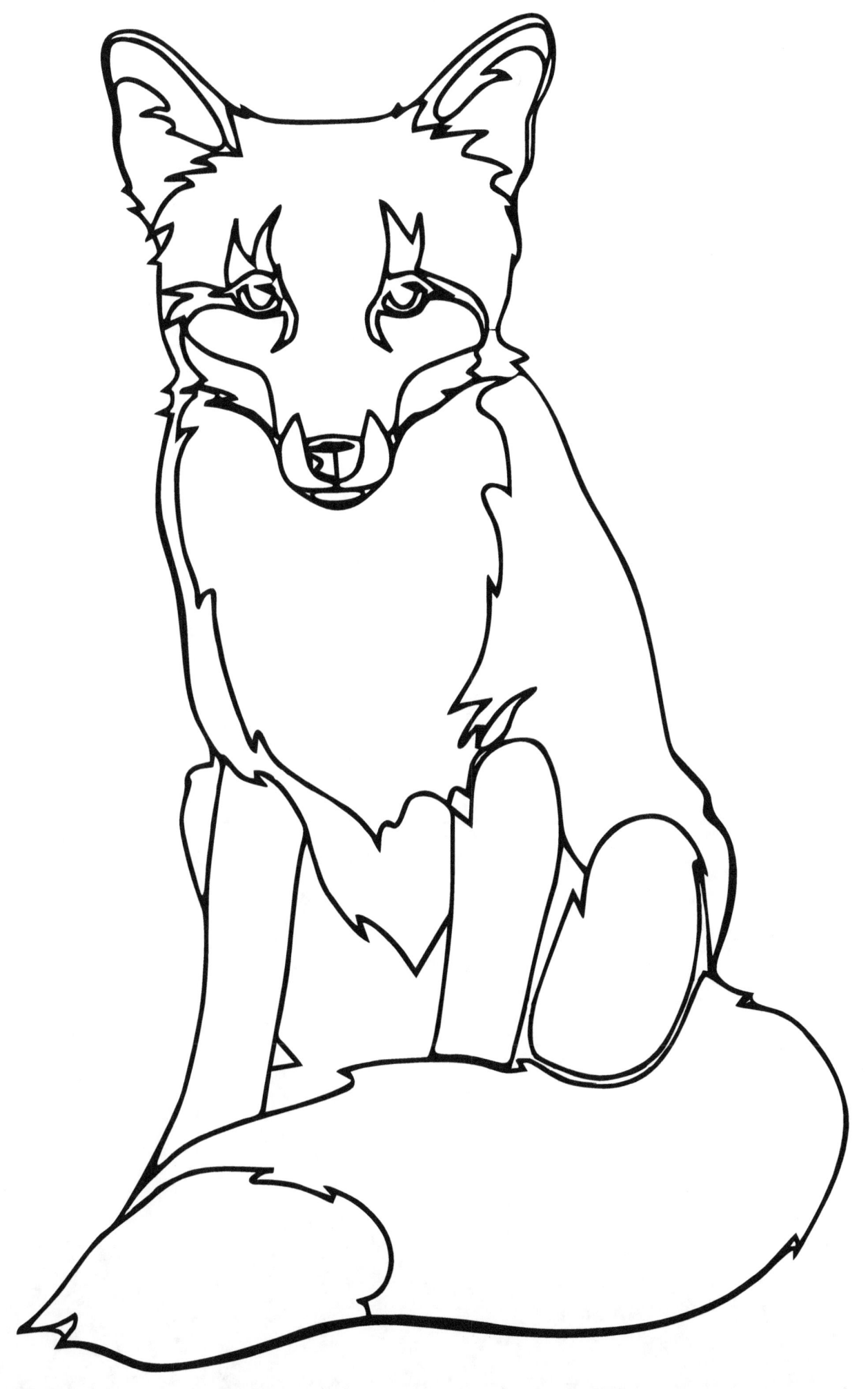

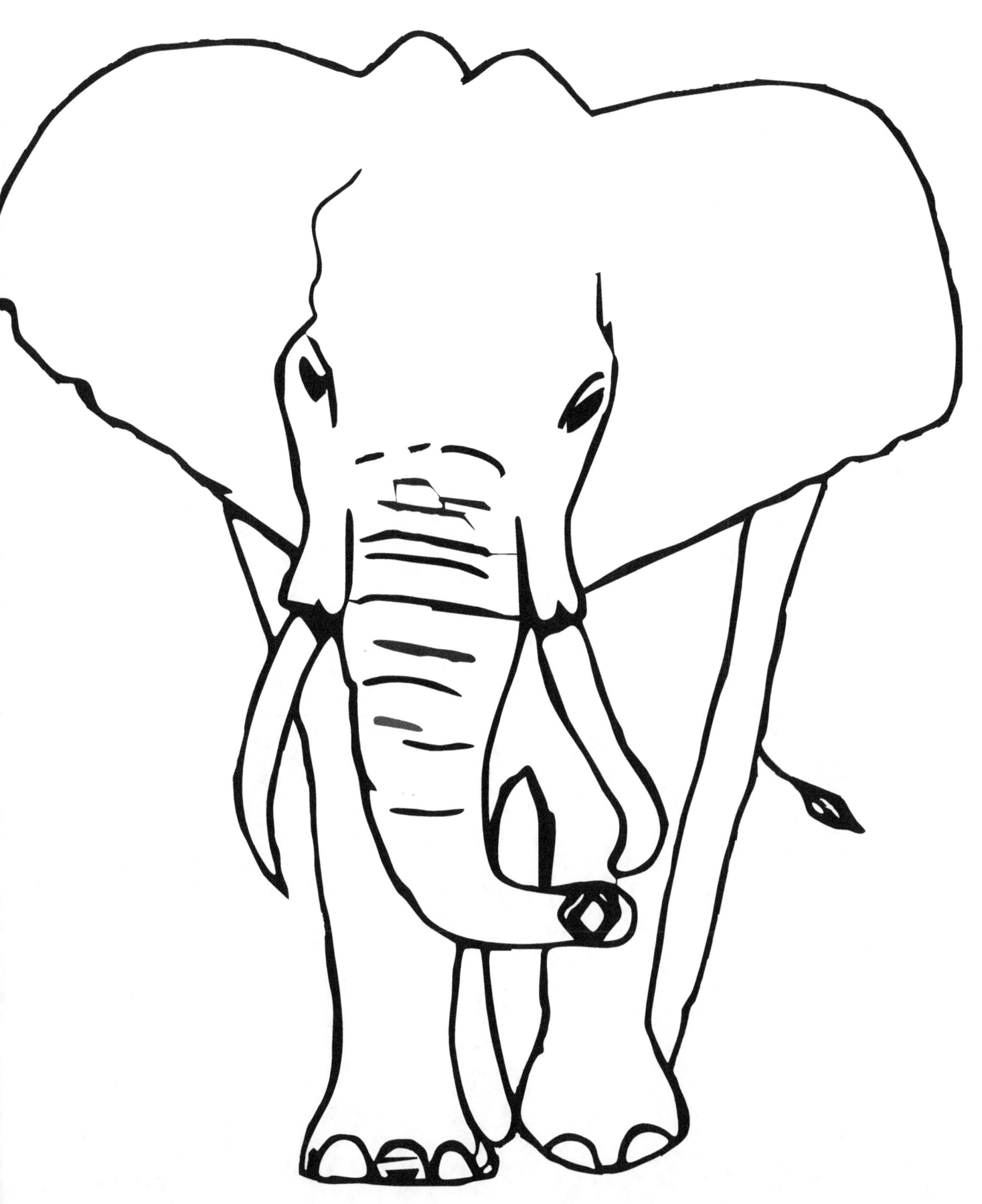

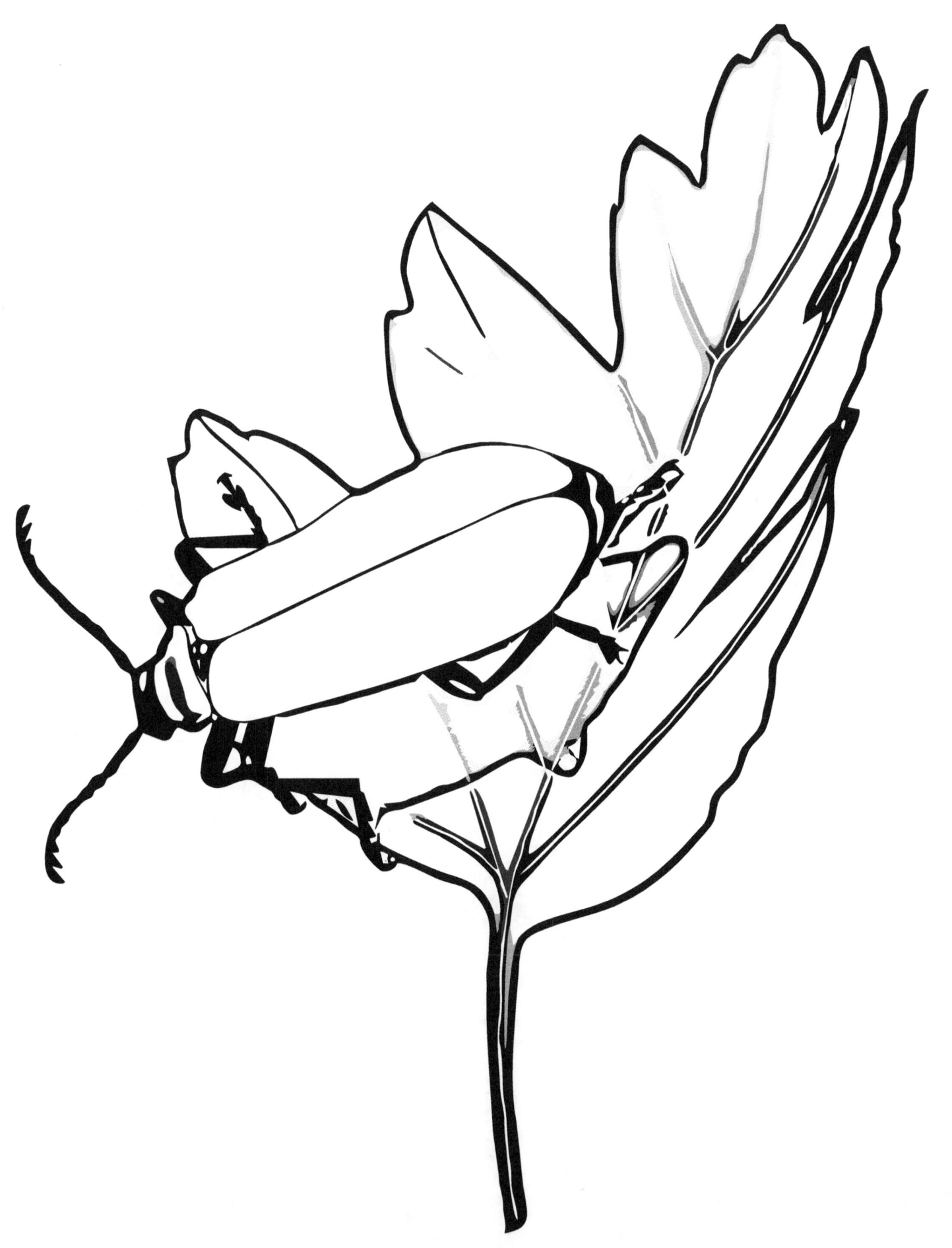

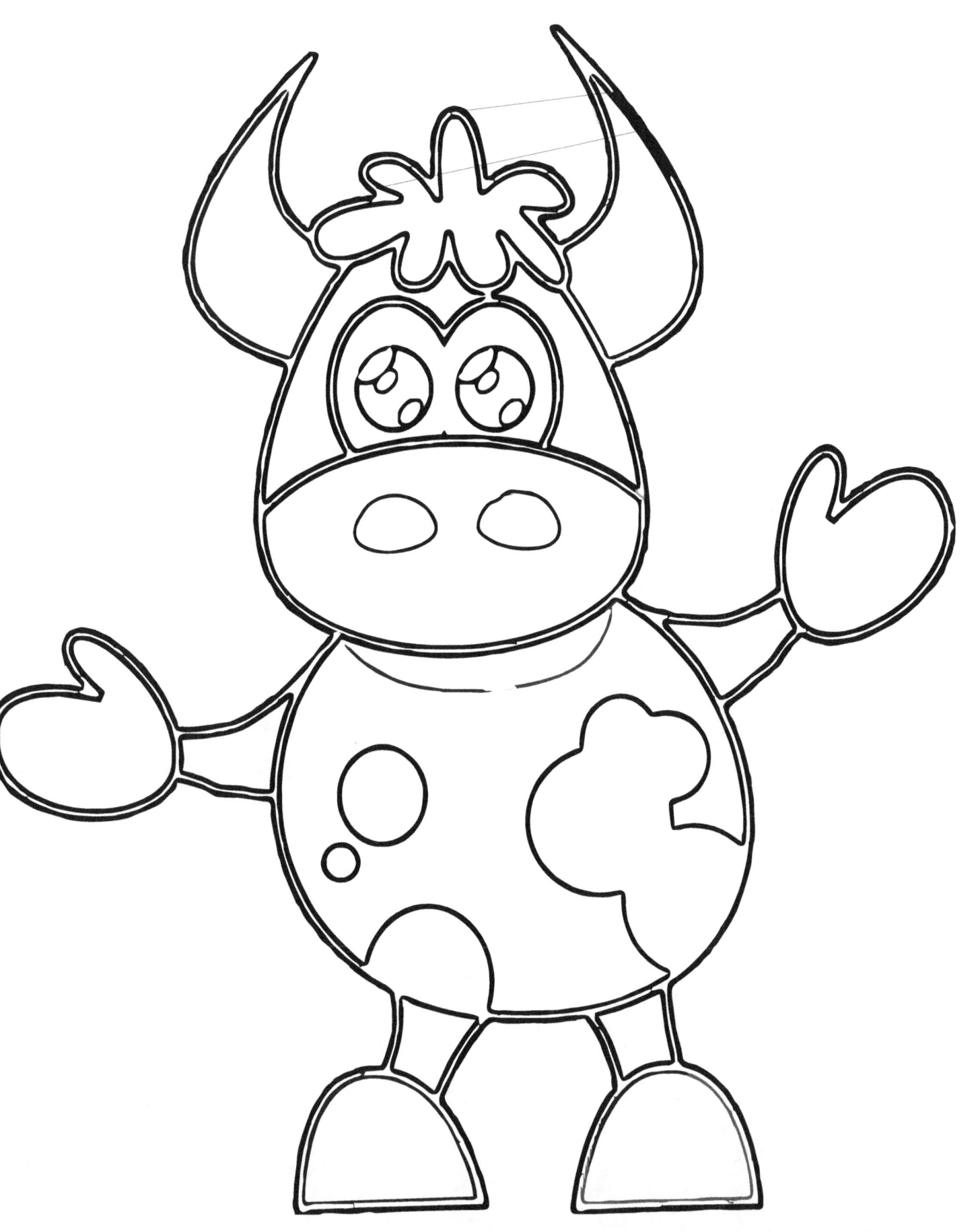

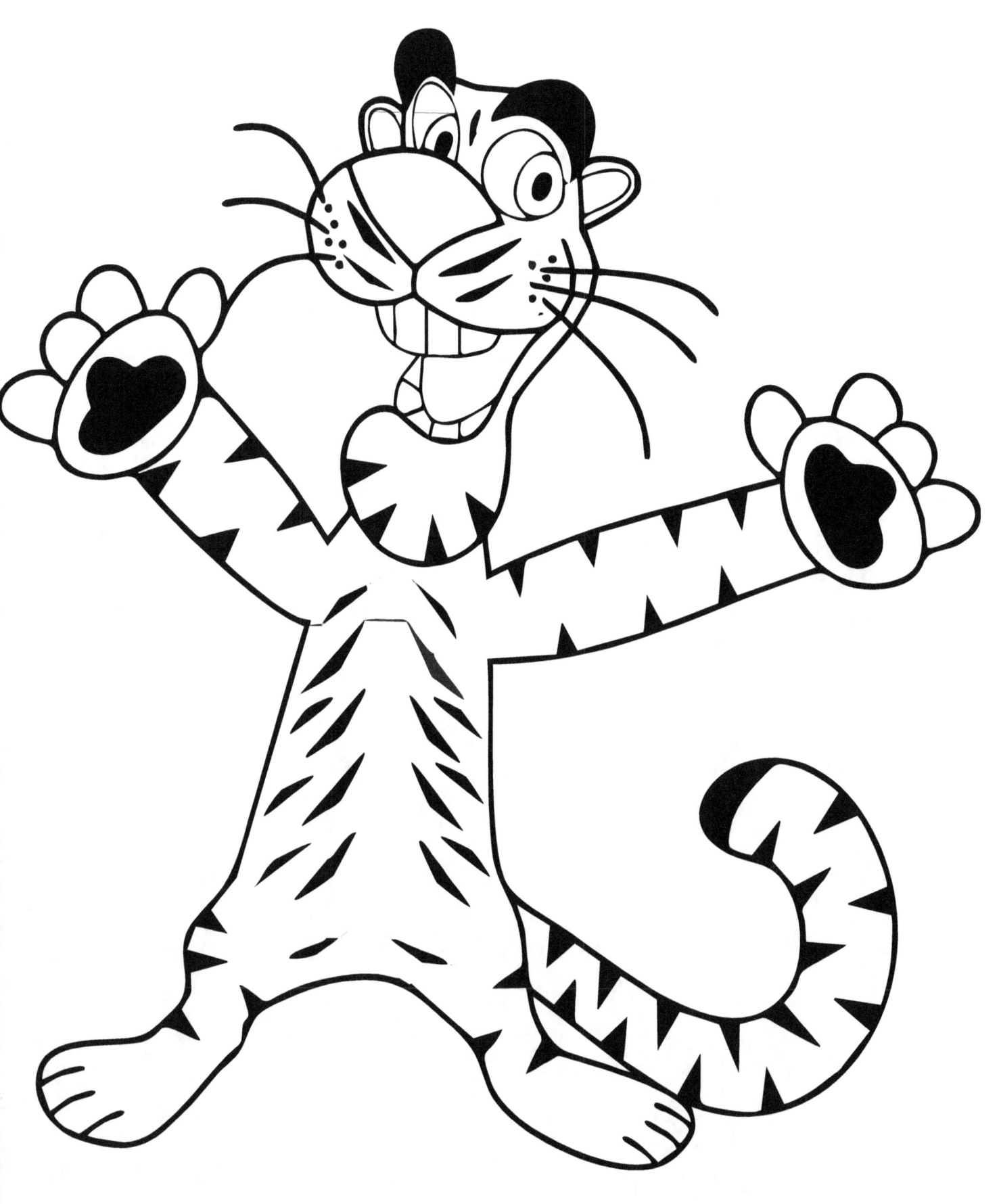

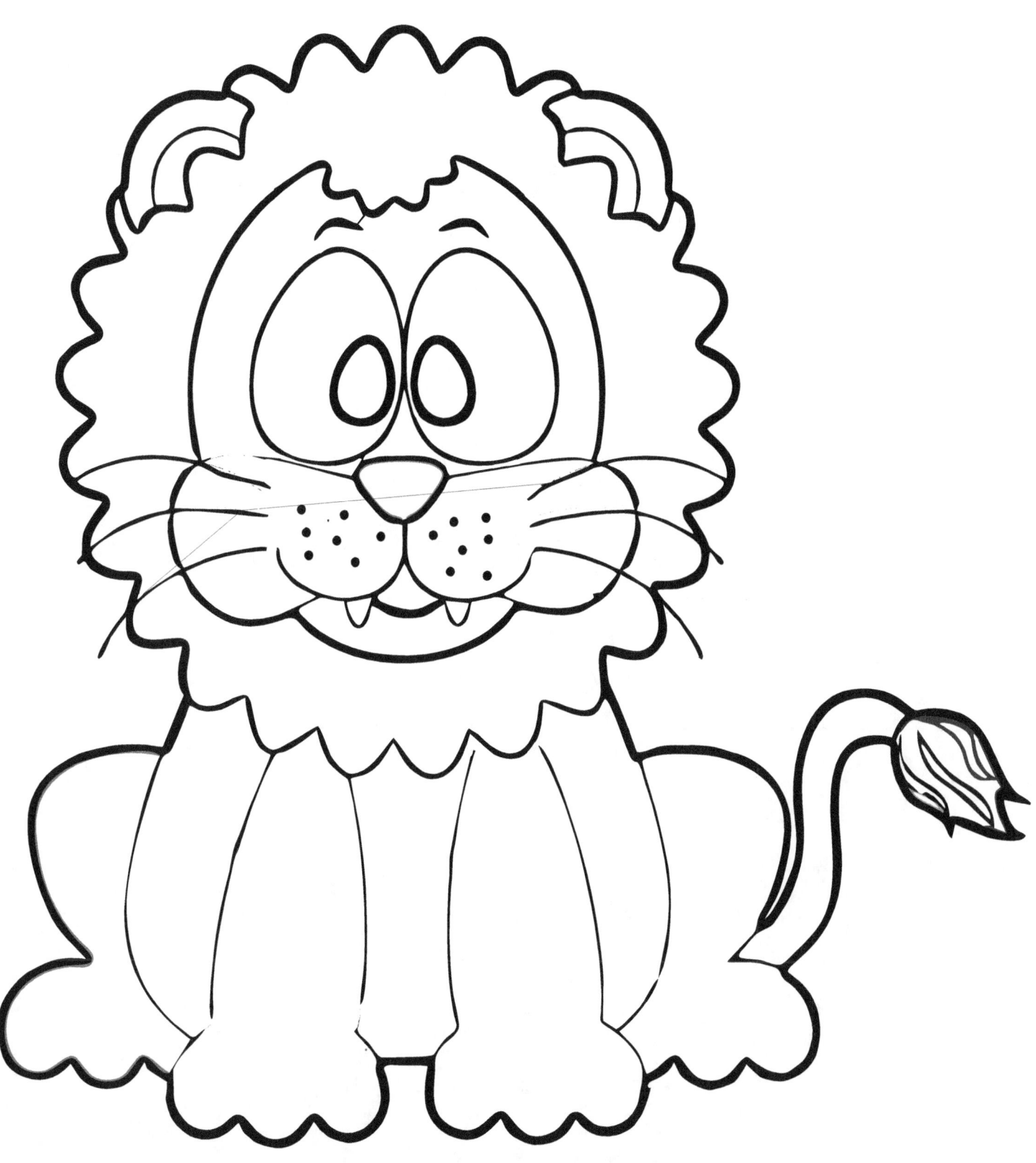

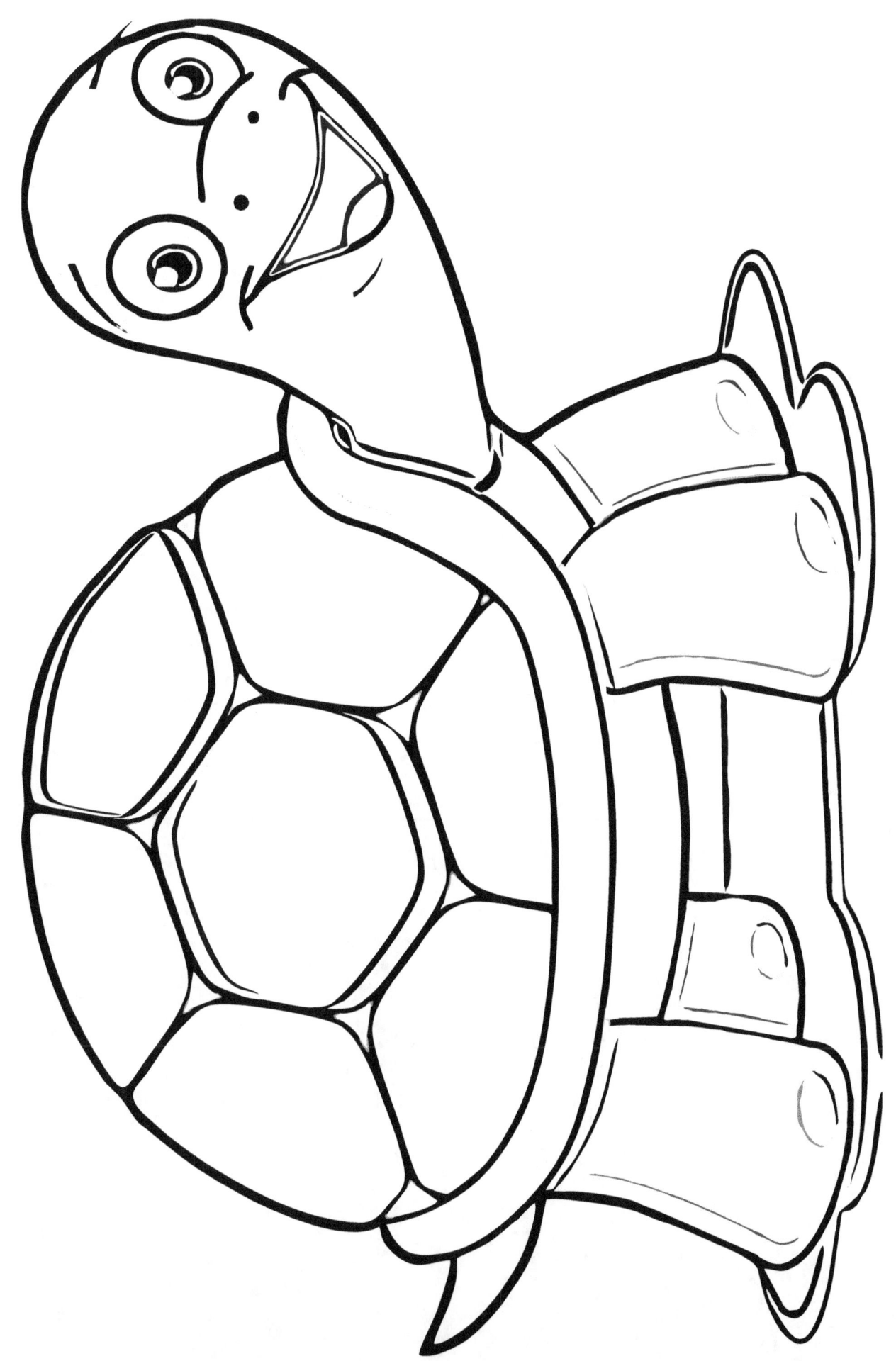

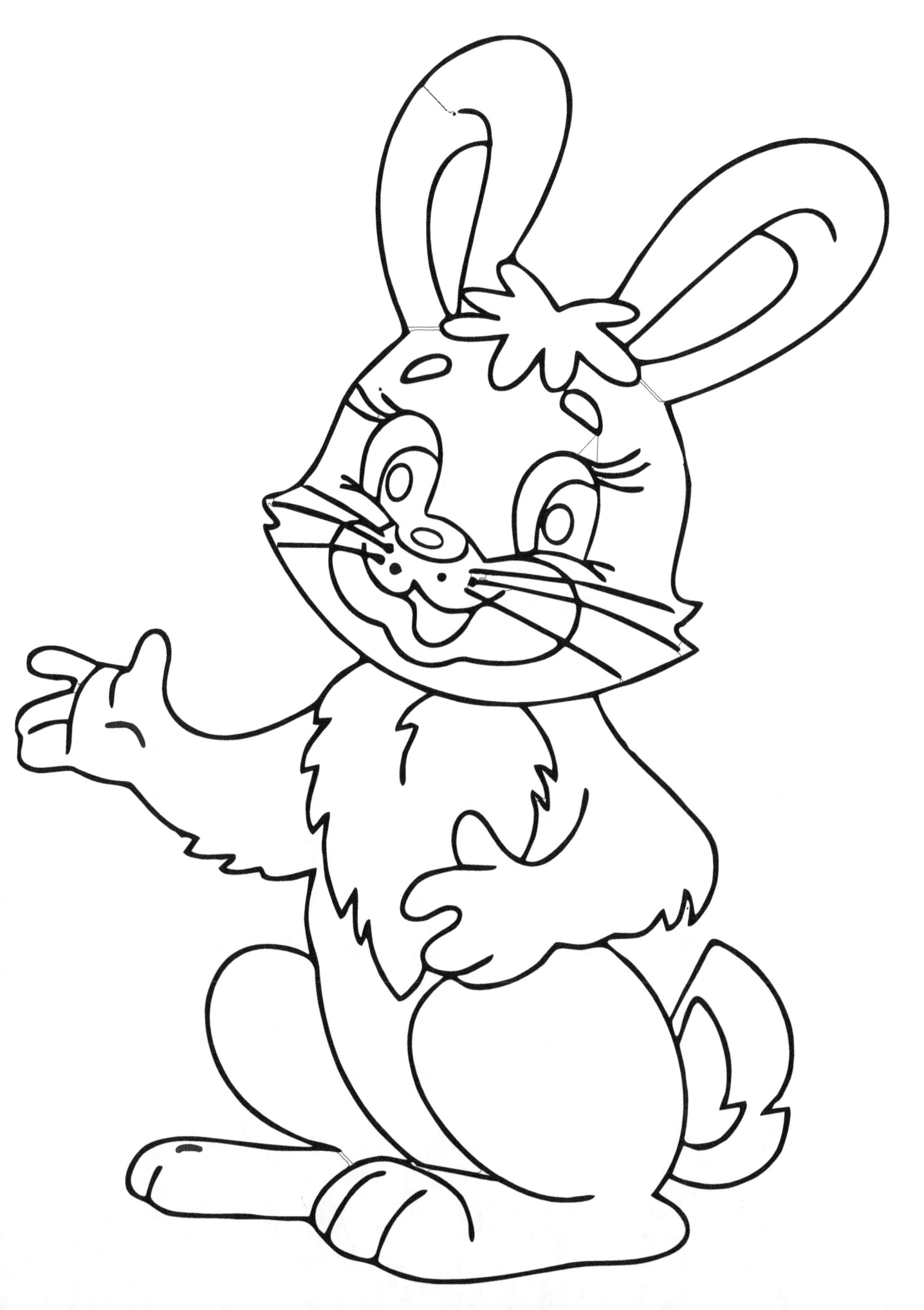

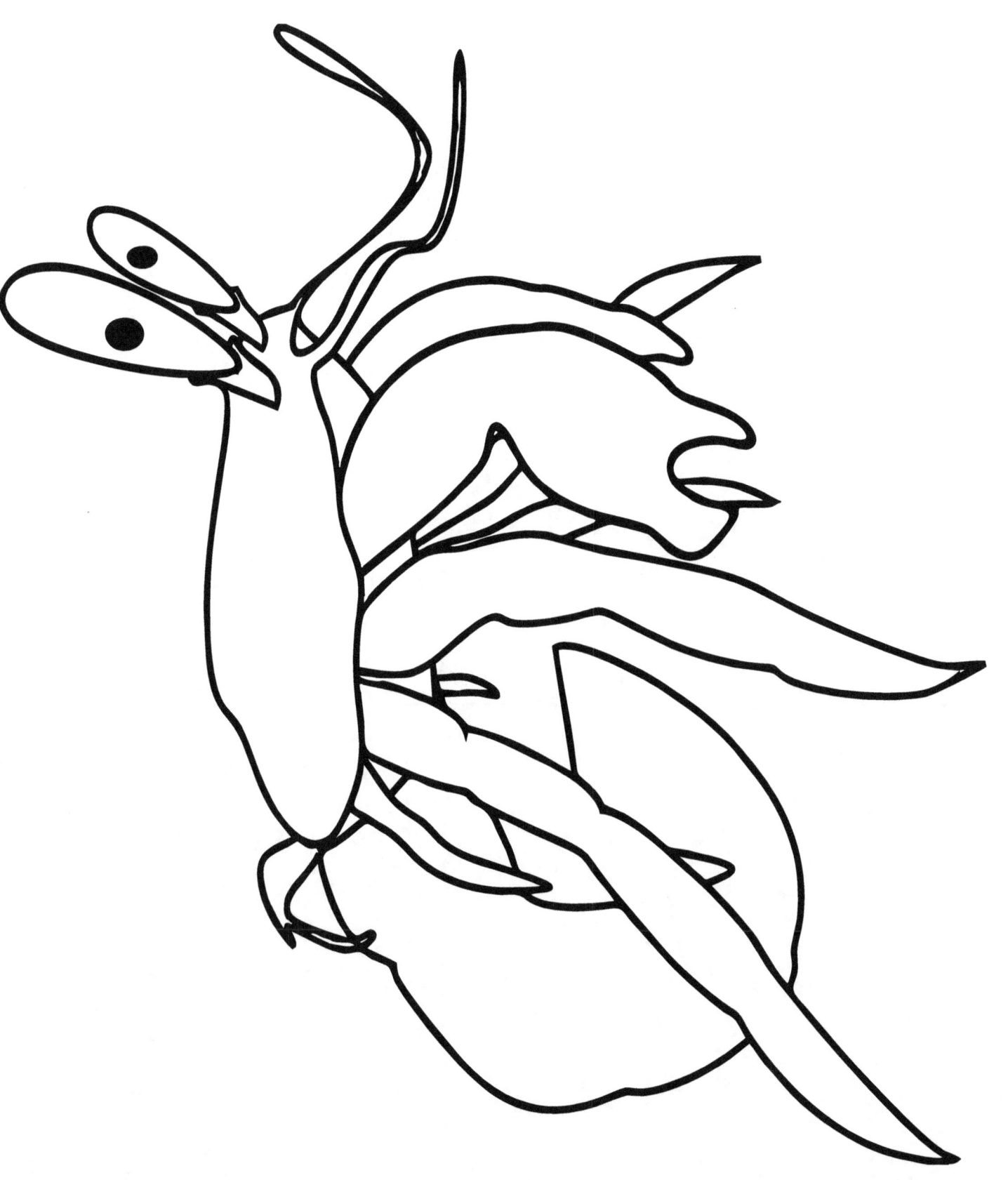

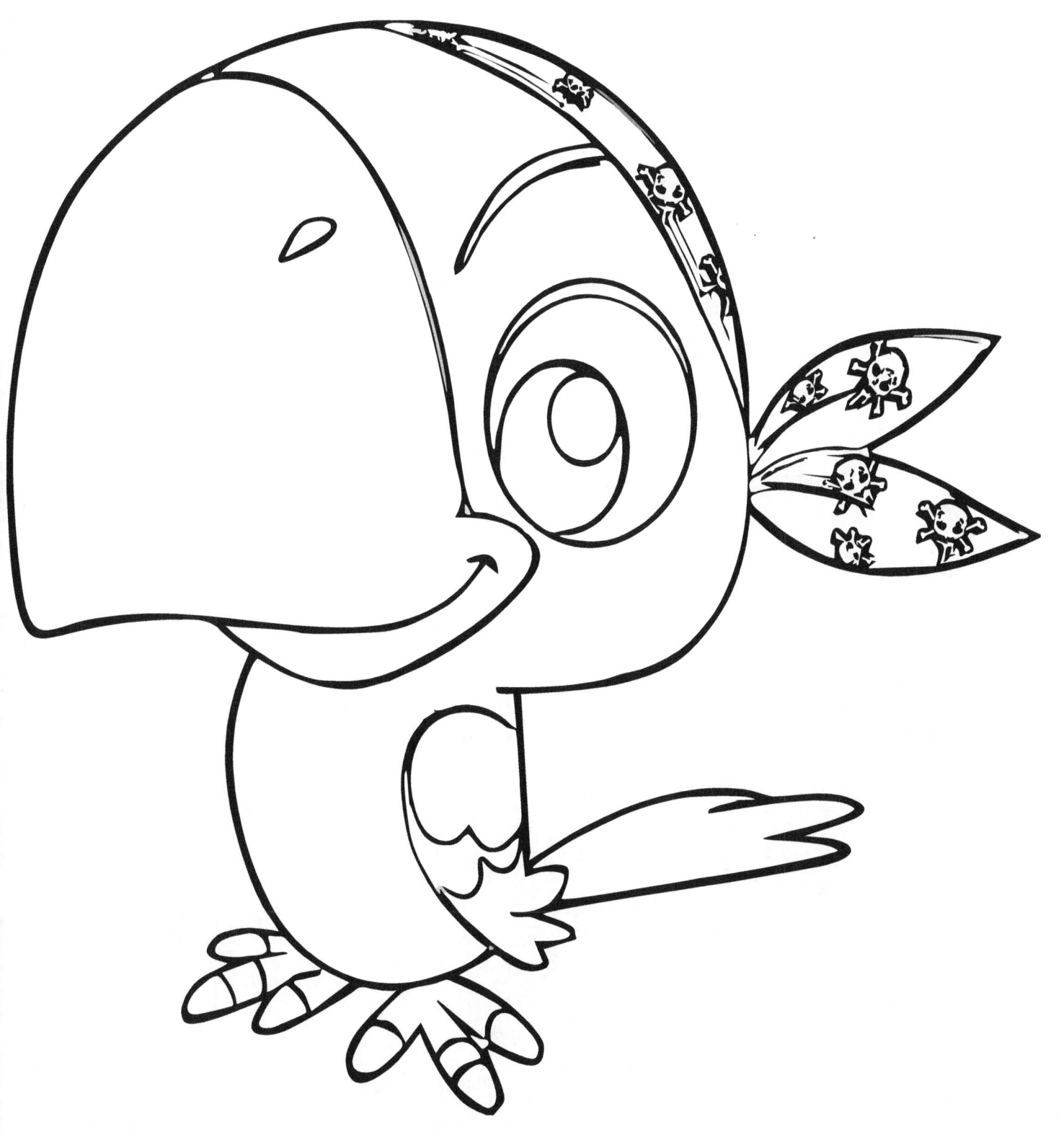

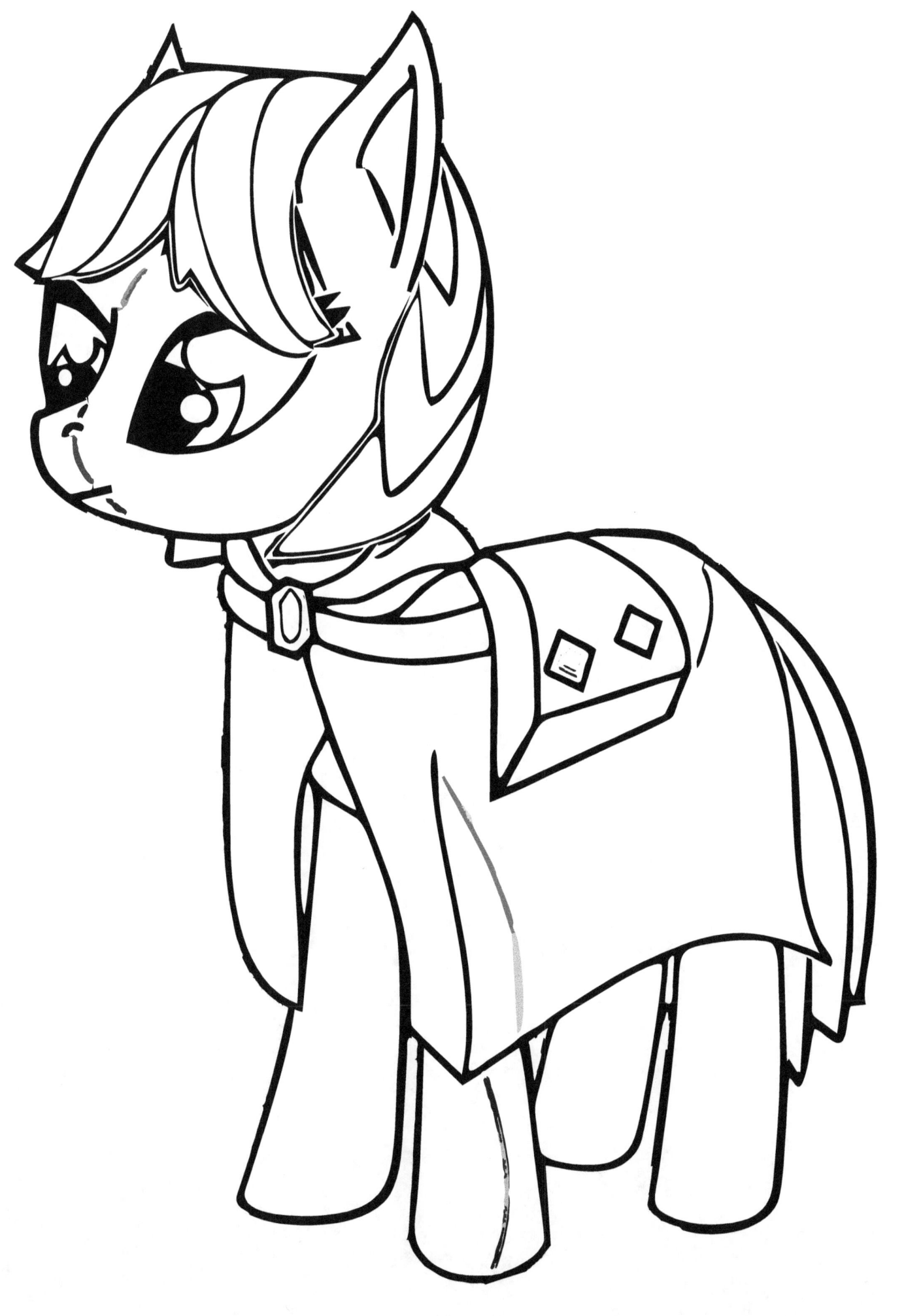

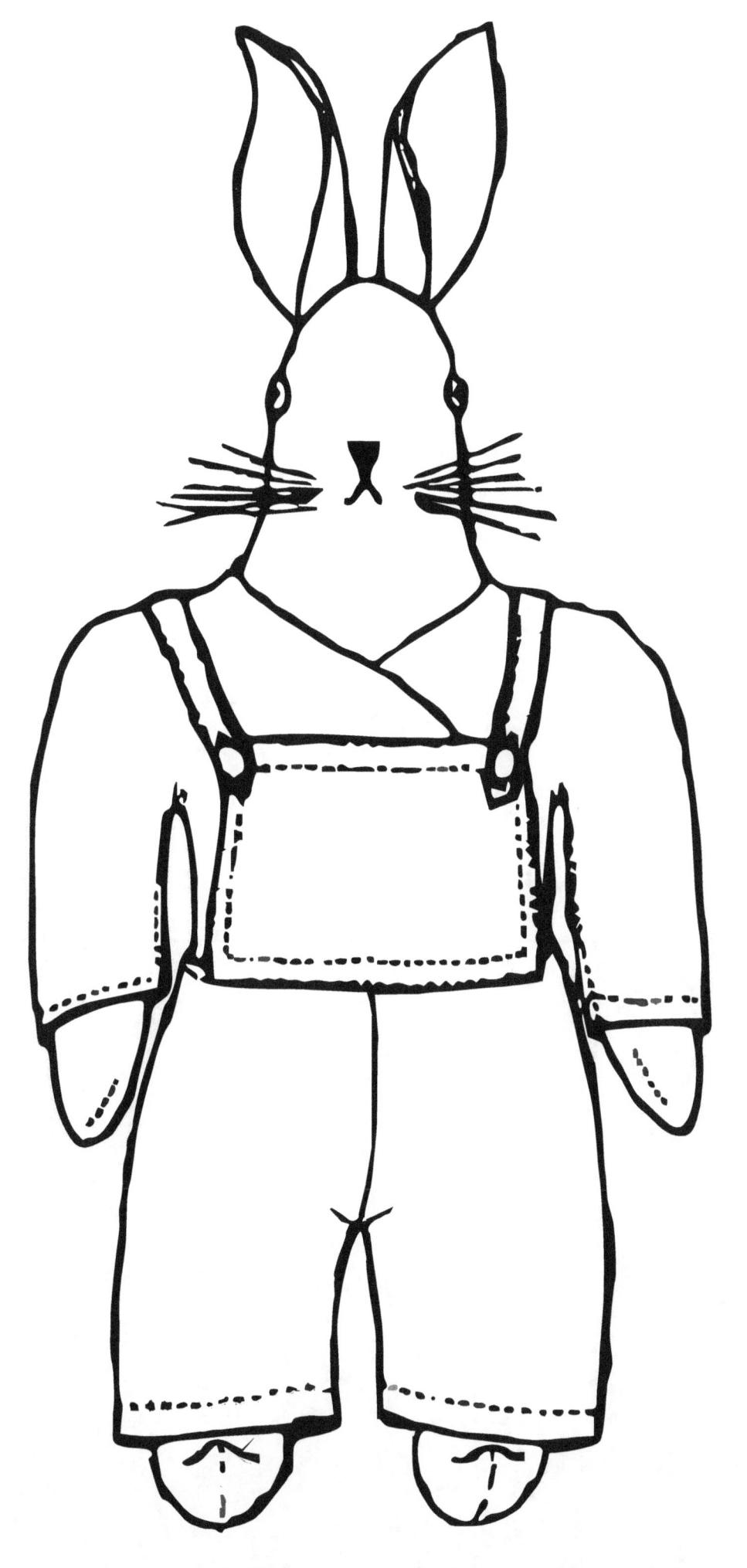

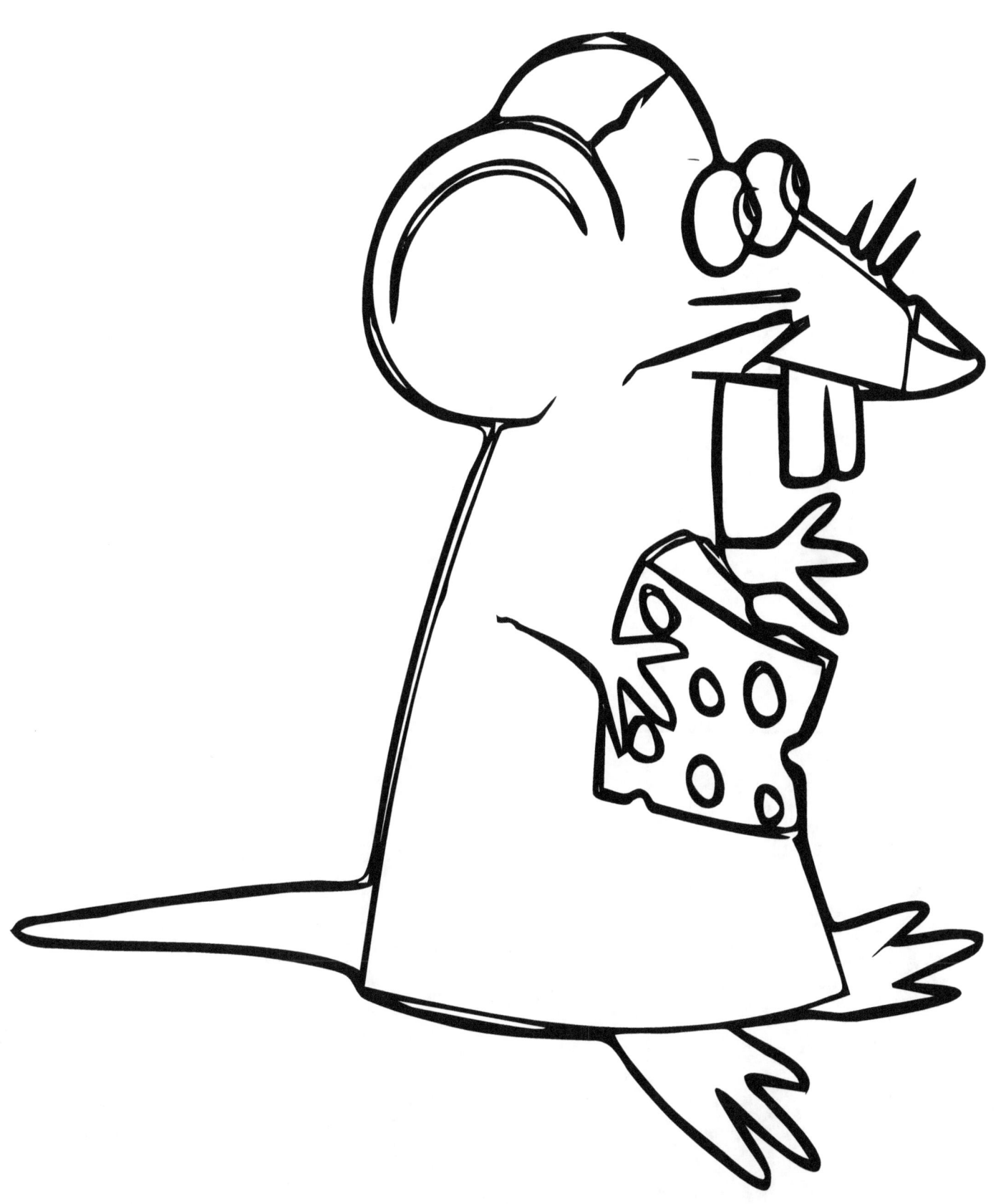

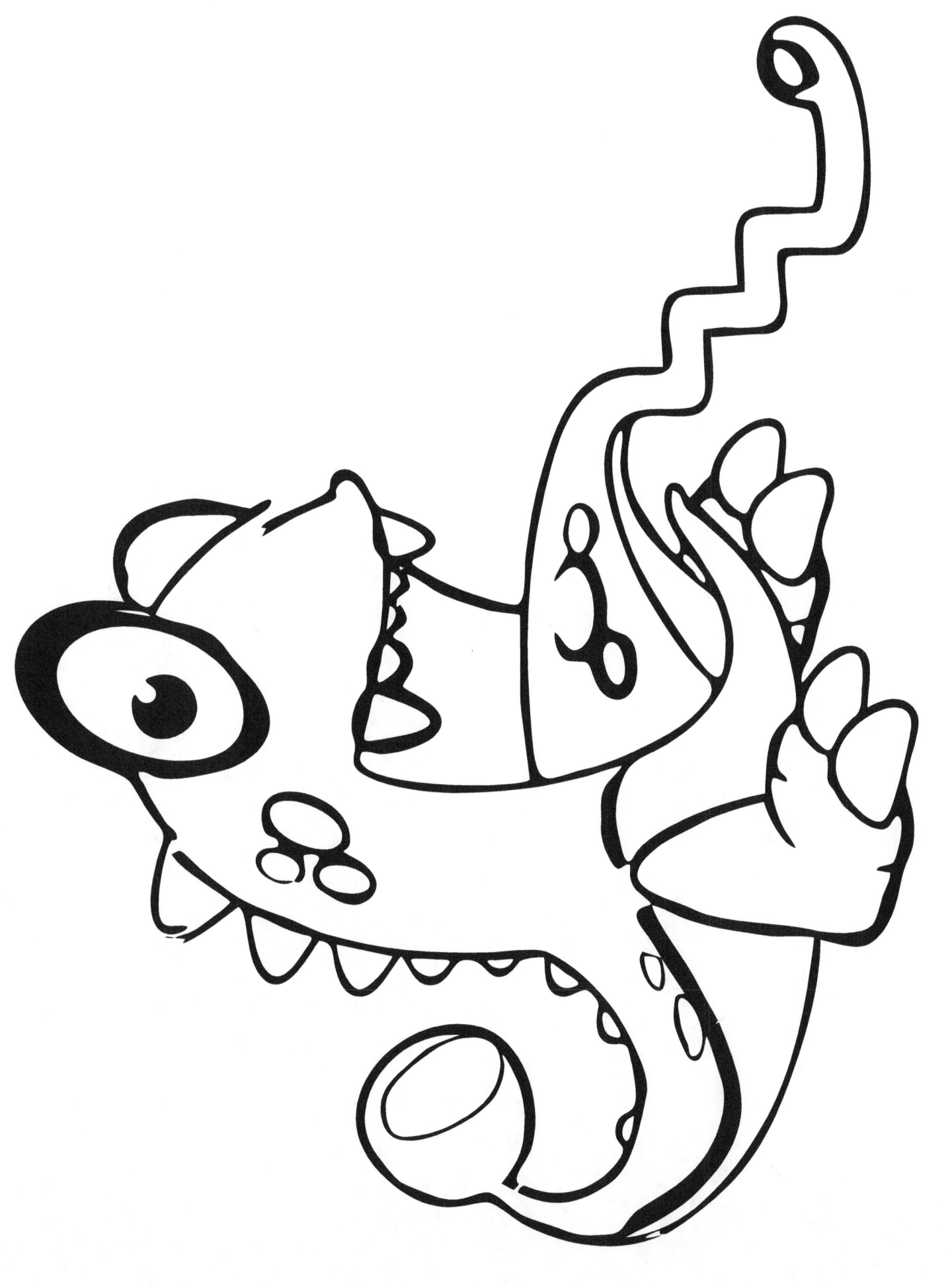

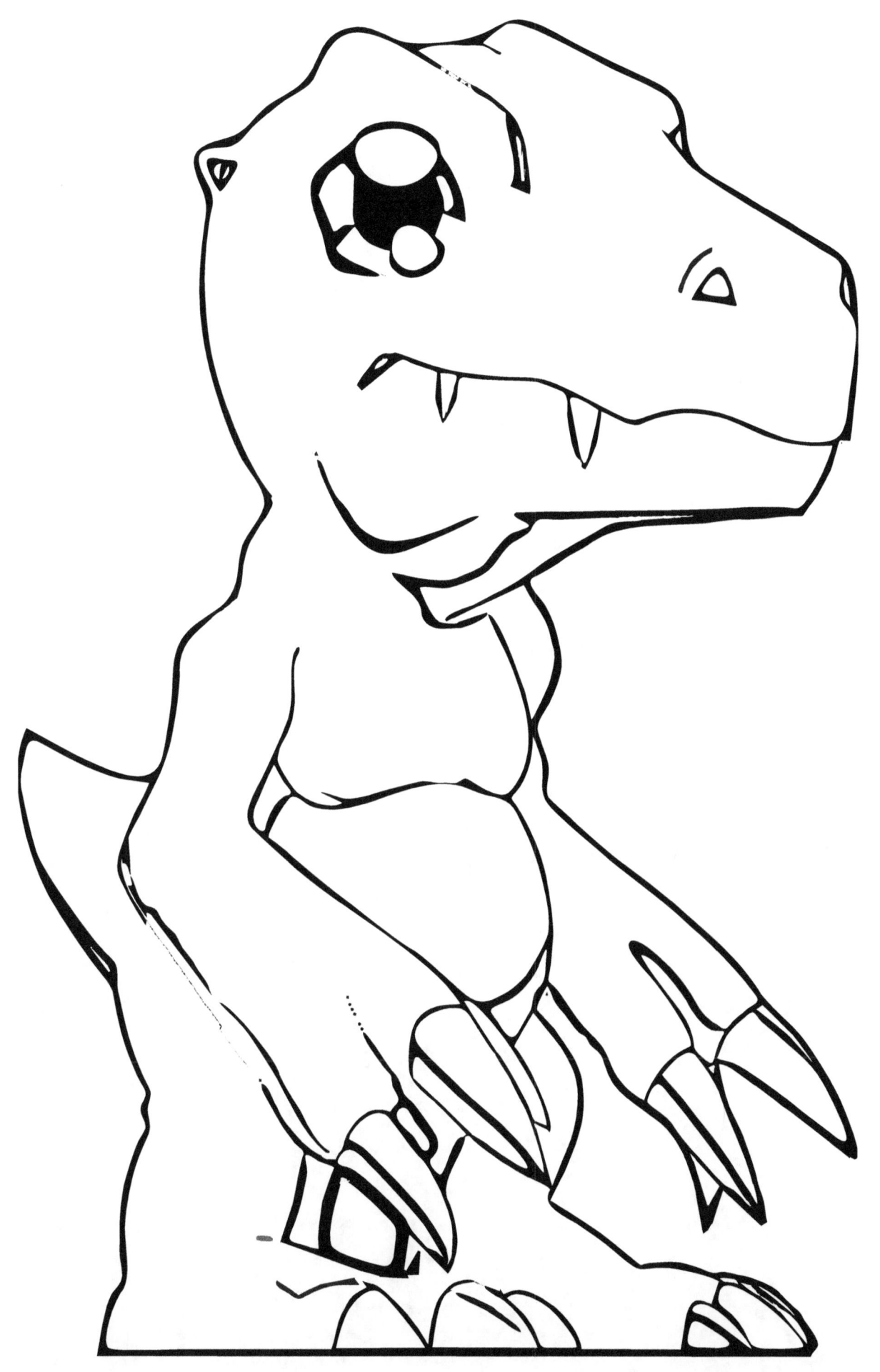

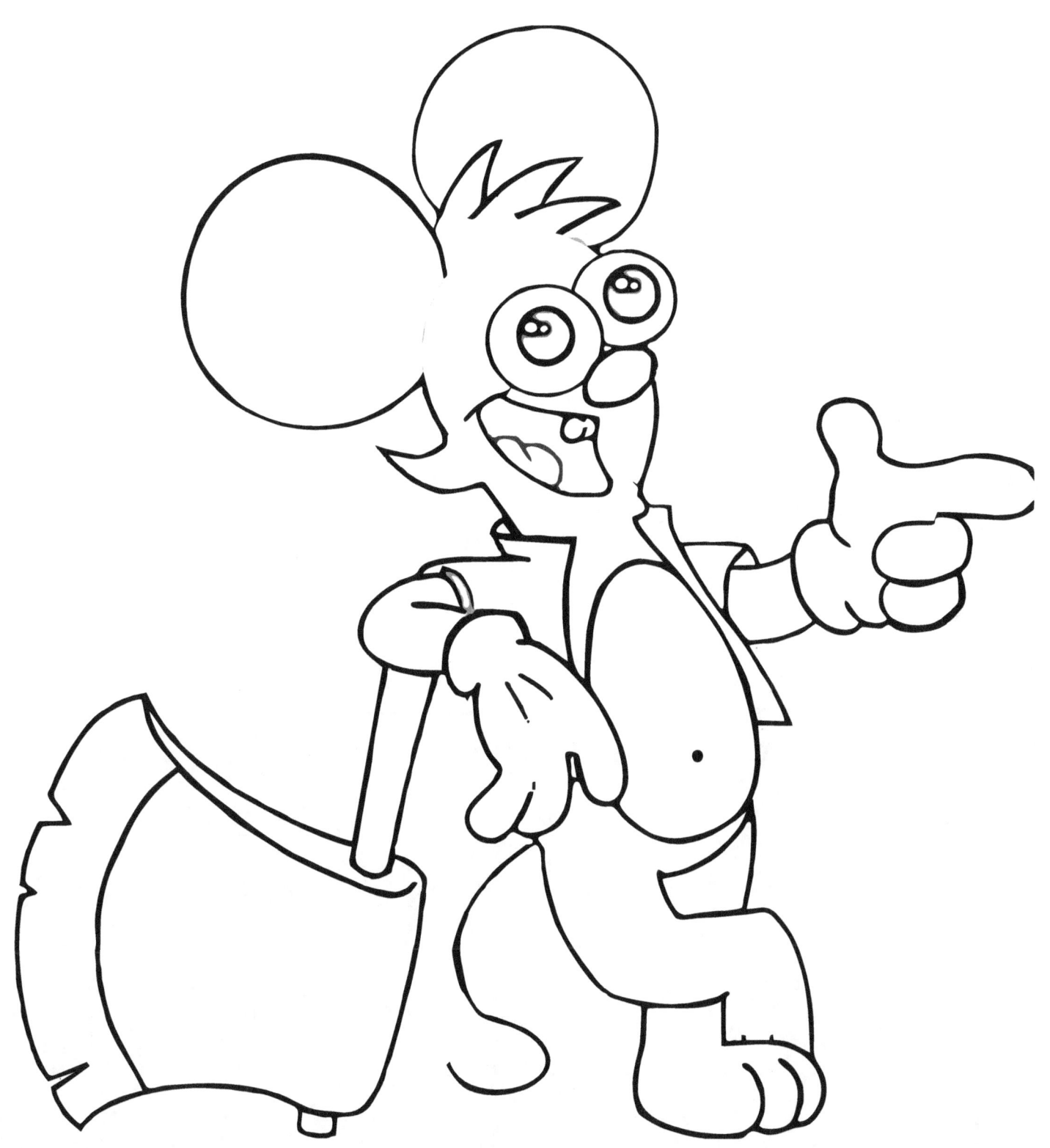

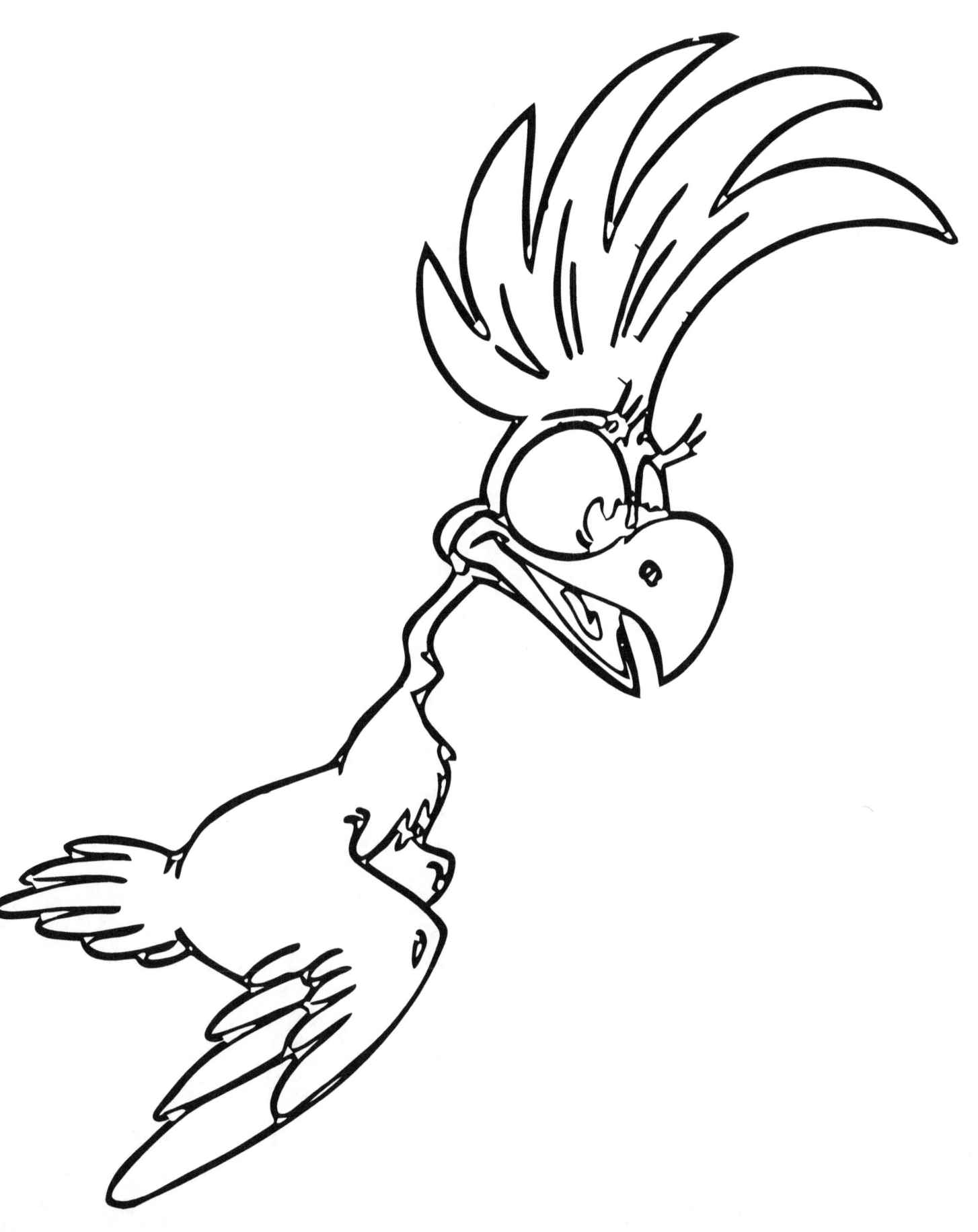

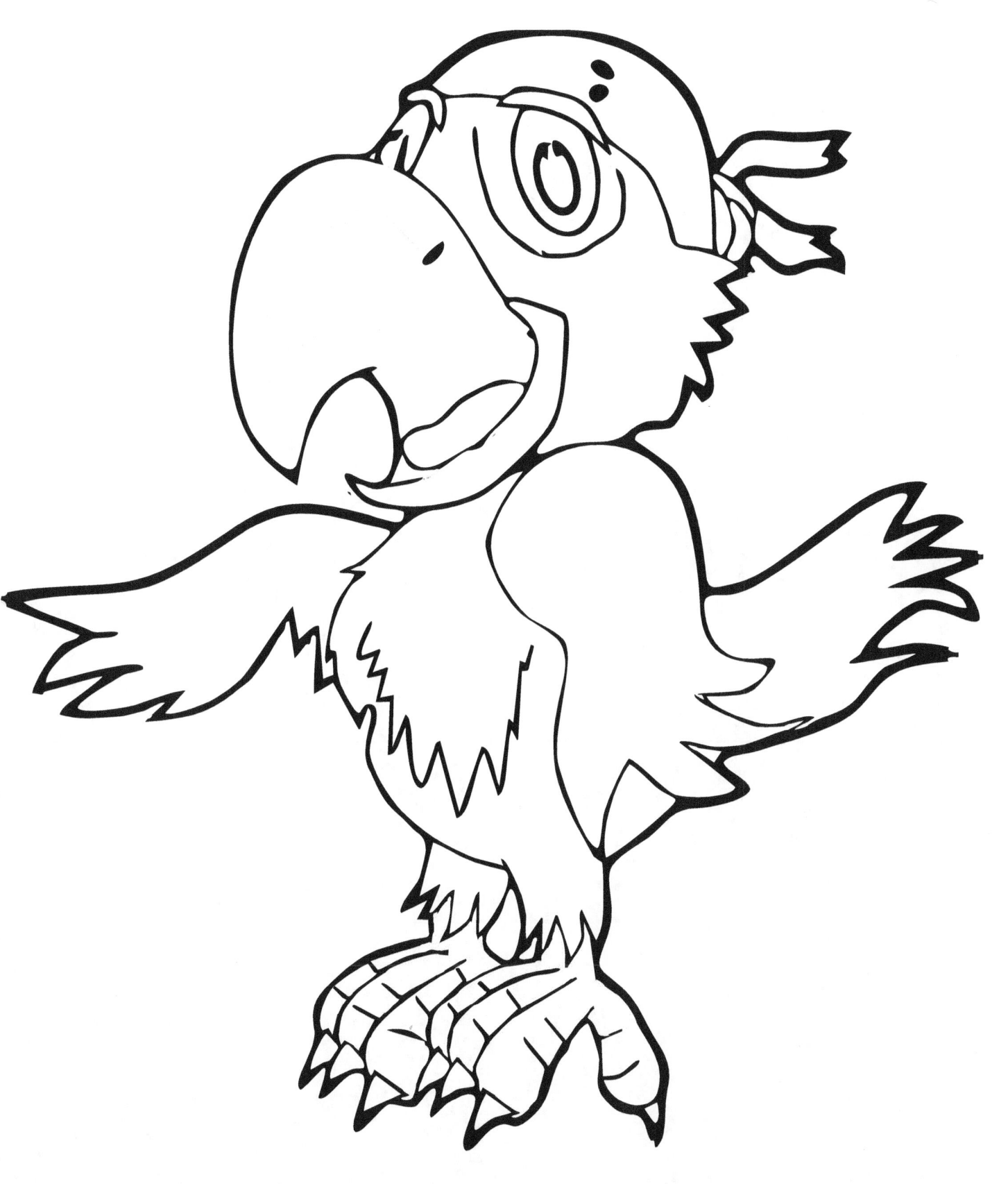

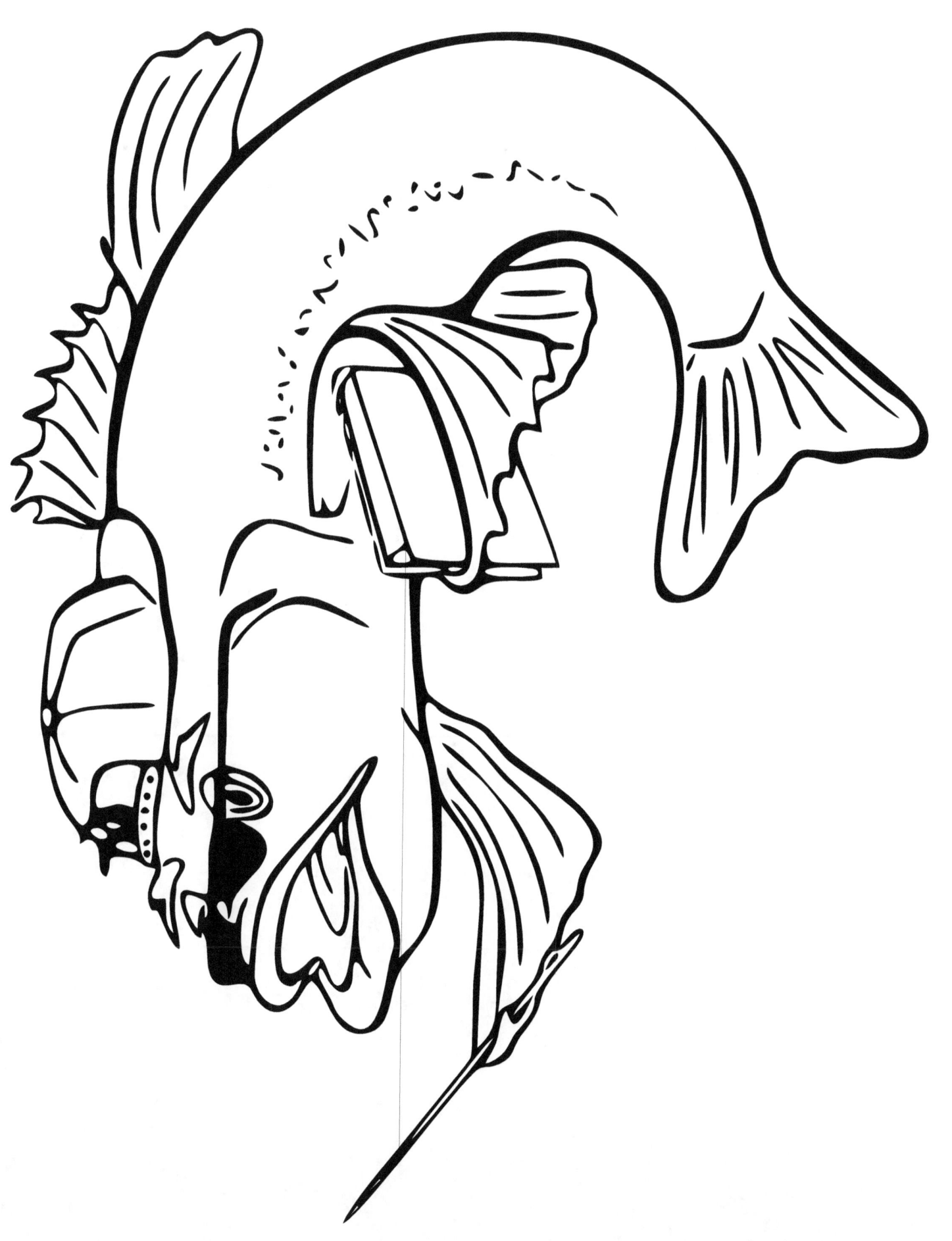

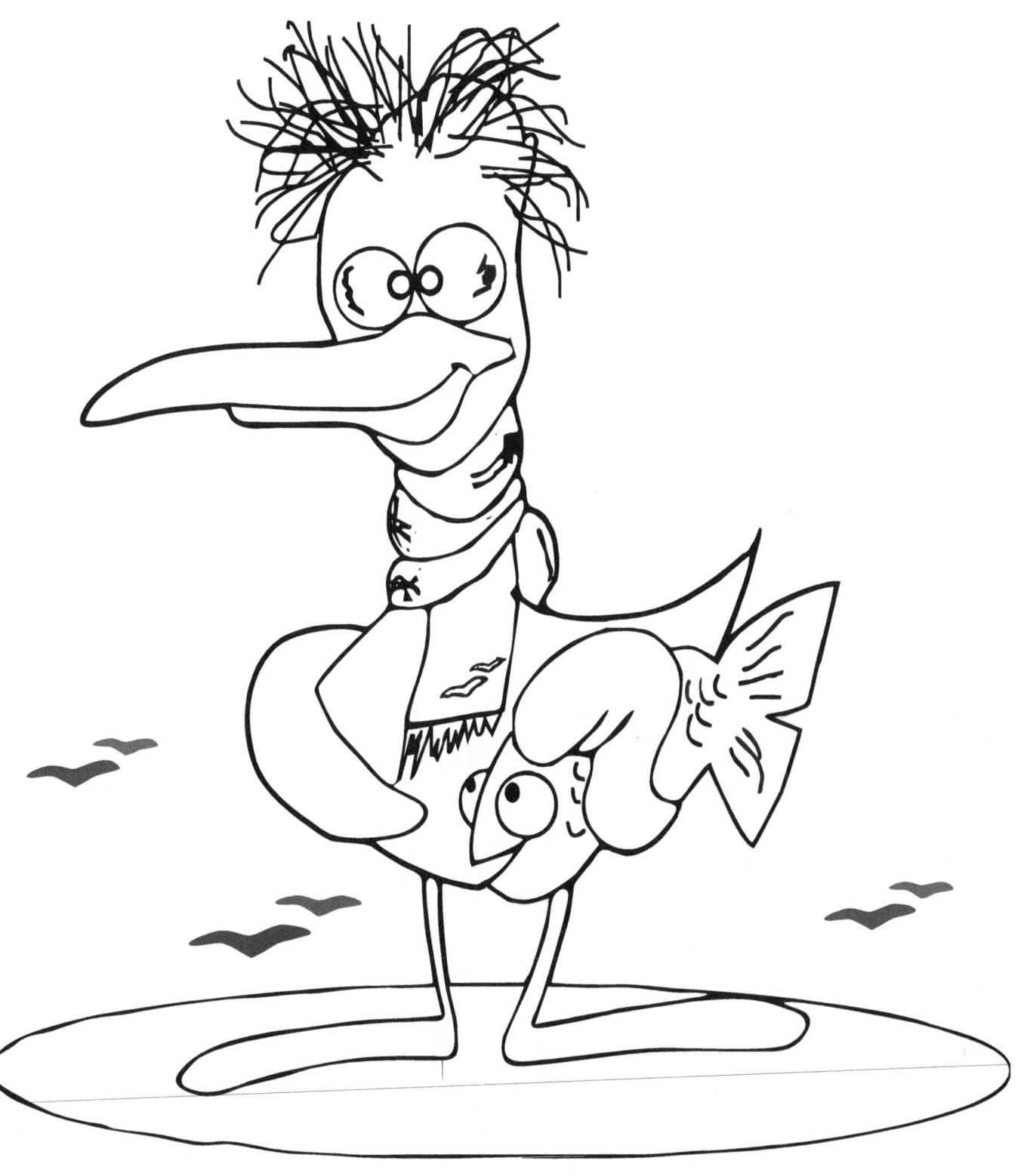

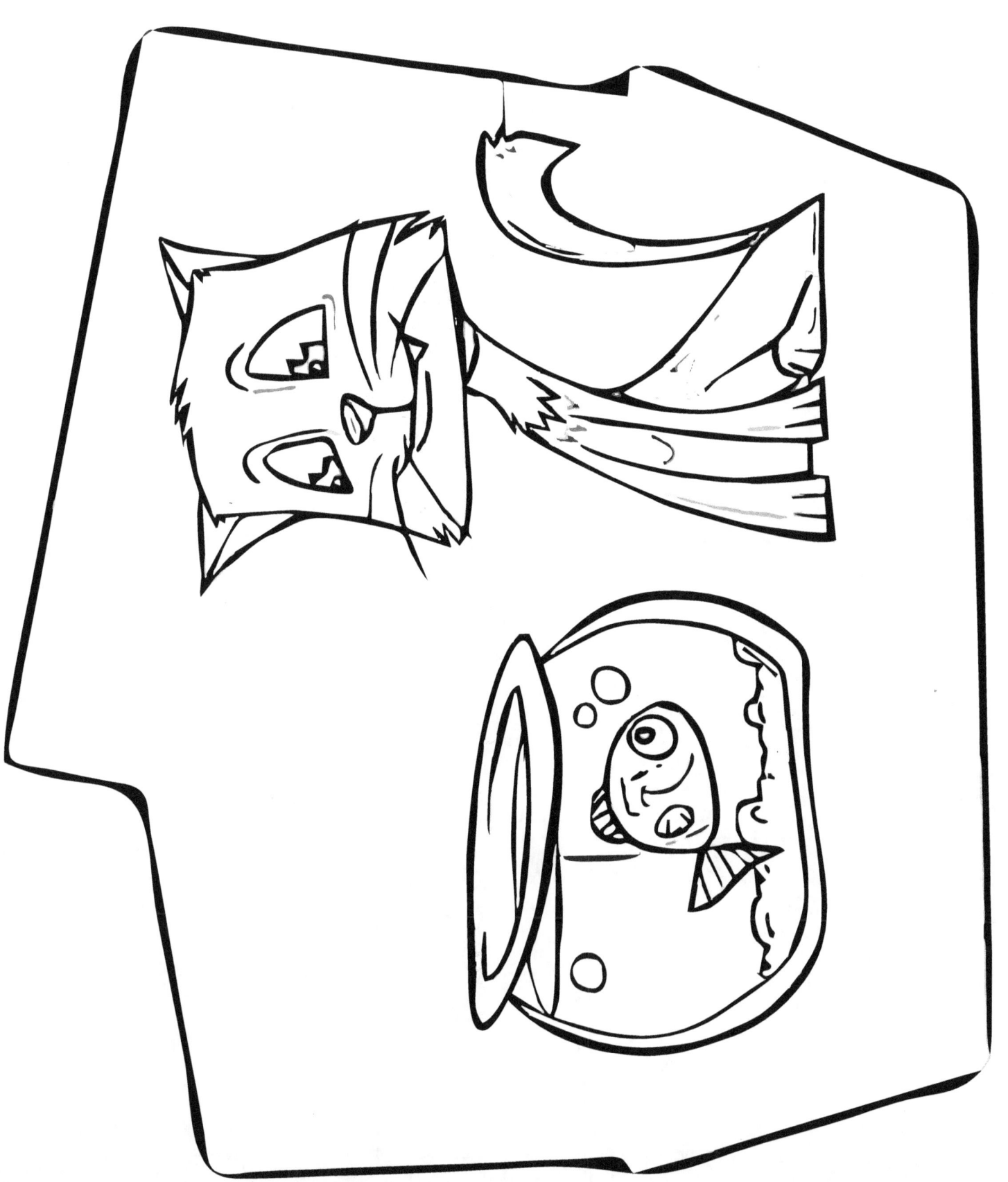

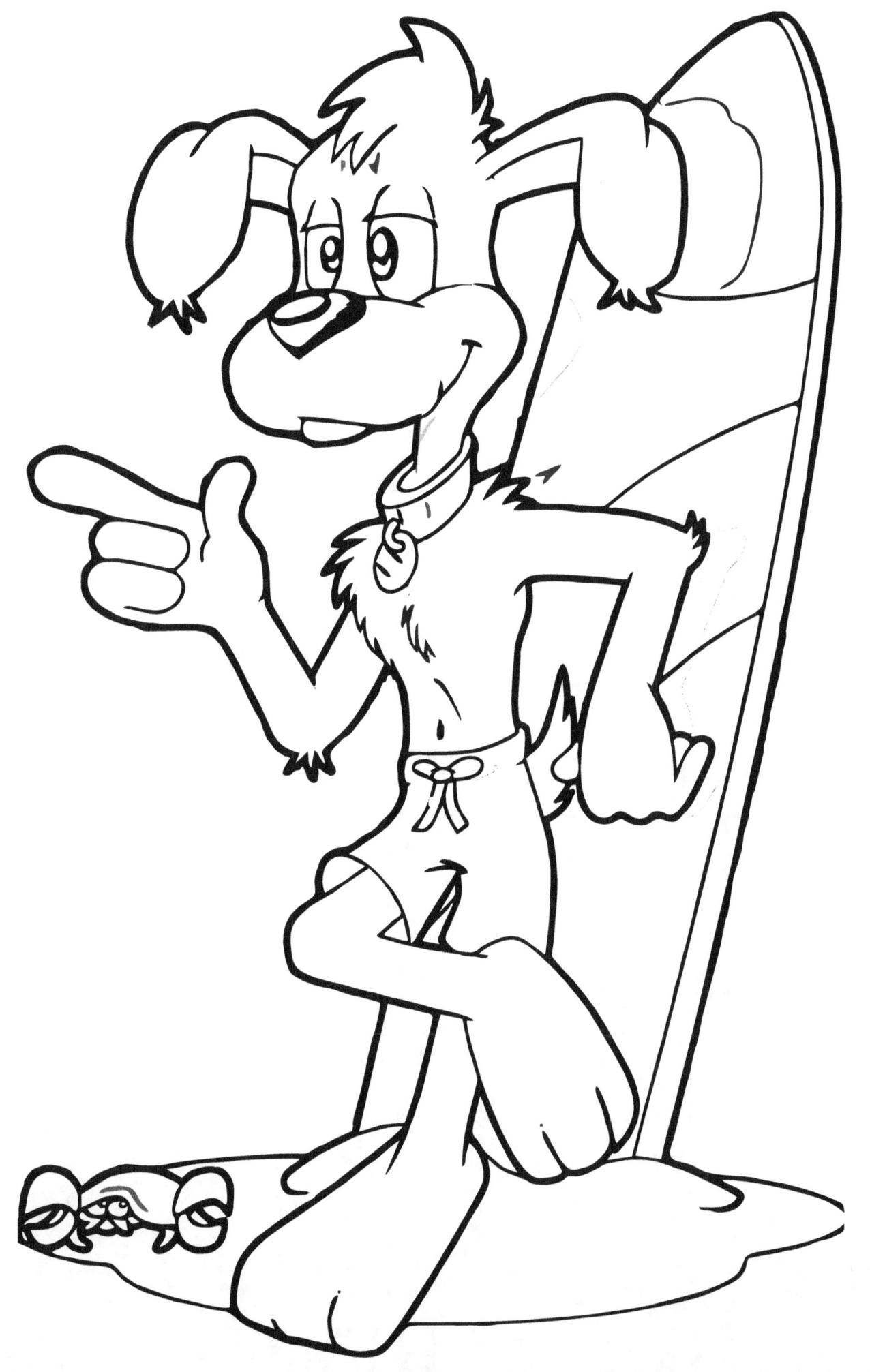

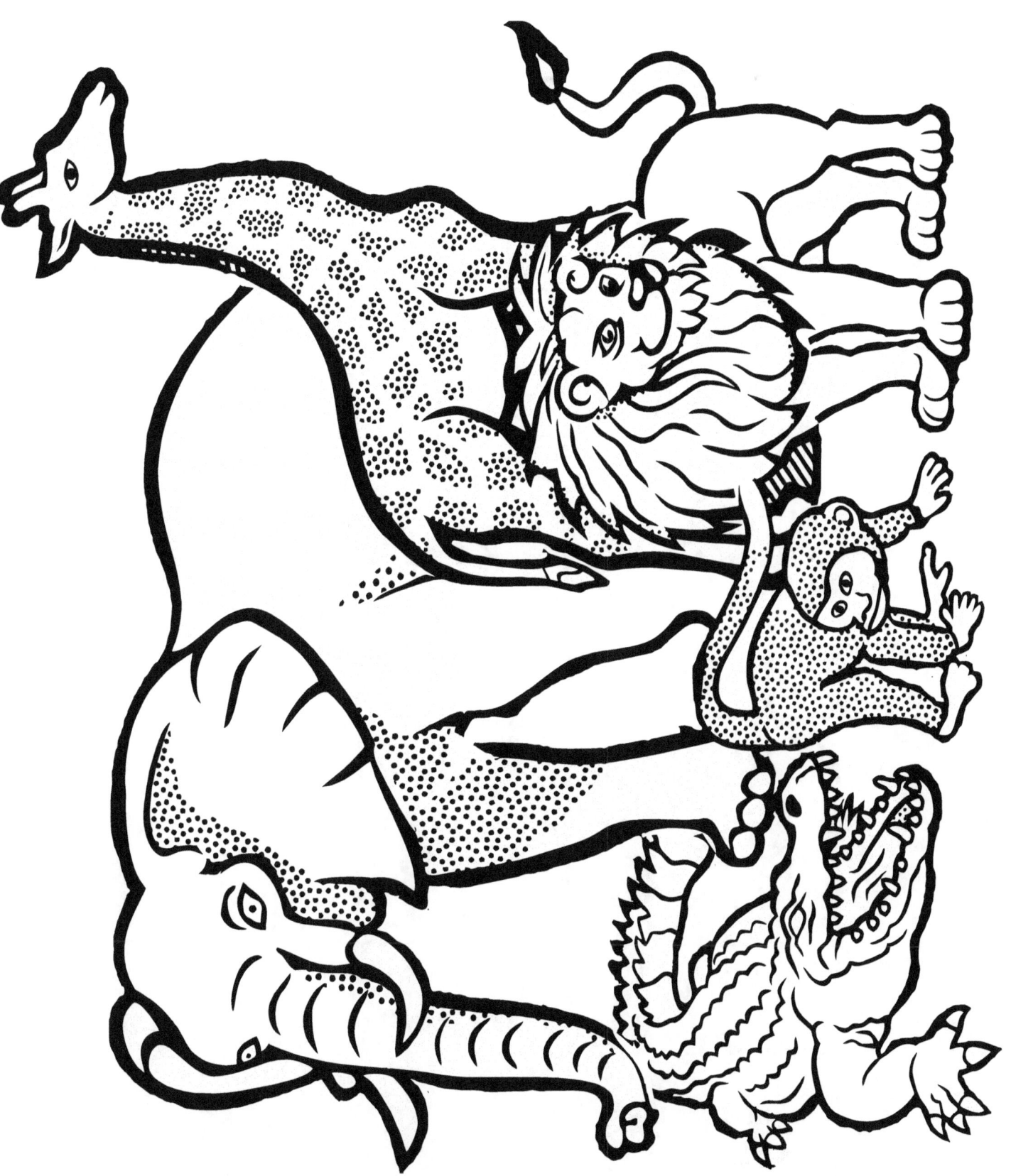

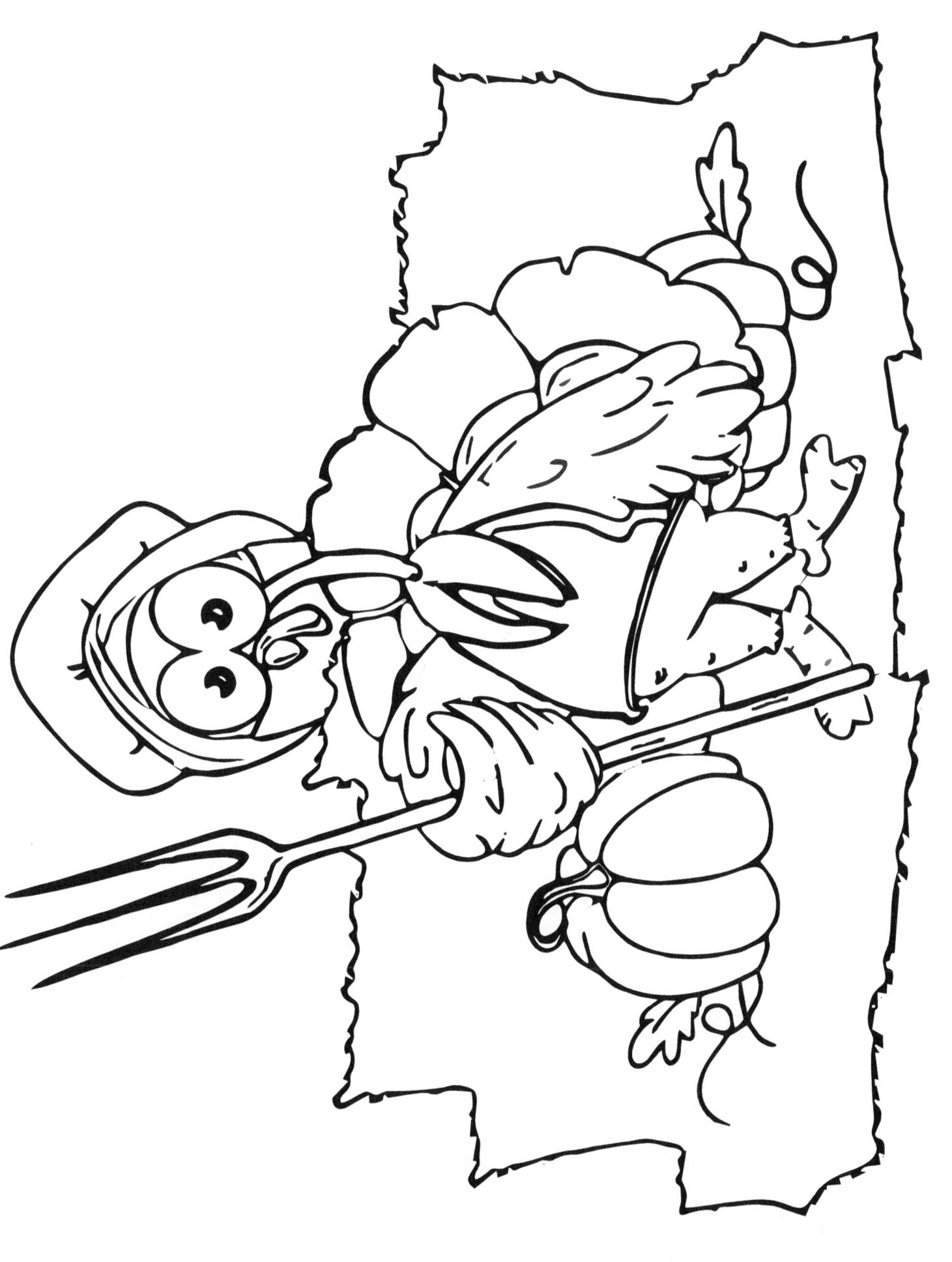

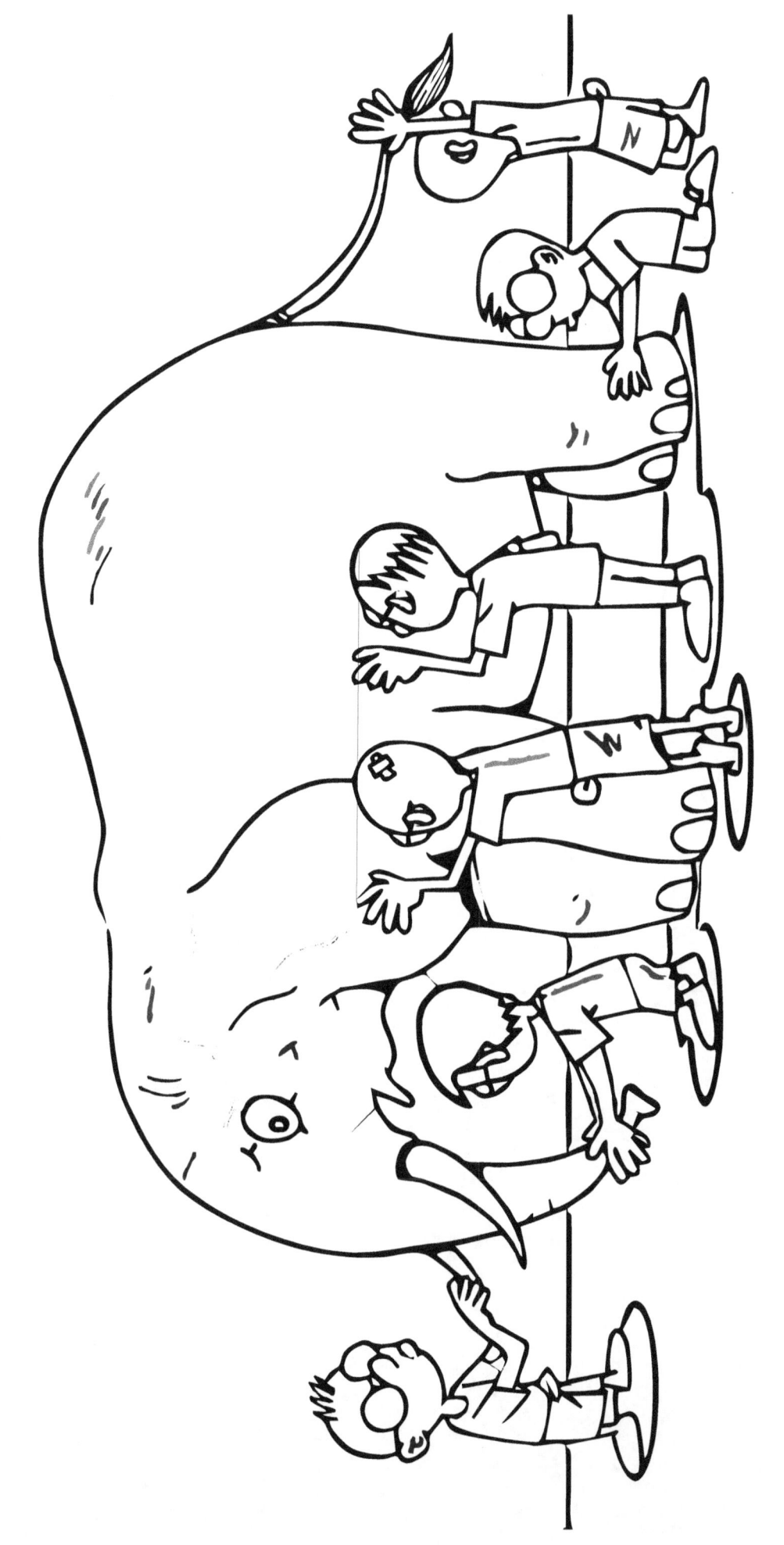

I will be very pleased if you and your child enjoy the time spent in this book colorings. Especially good if at the same time will benefit to the development of attention, motor skills and perseverance of your child. I will be glad to do much good colorings for you !. **THANK YOU!**

Emily Green

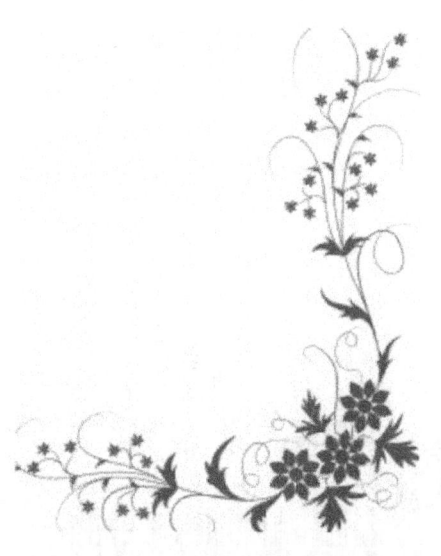

2017

www.ingramcontent.com/pod-product-compliance
Lightning Source LLC
Chambersburg PA
CBHW080308180526
45167CB00006B/2718